"As a member of the World Champion Dallas Cowboys, Chad Hennings is in a position to influence our youth. He takes this role seriously, as he shares his experiences and Christian testimony in *It Takes Commitment*. *It Takes Commitment* teaches the importance of setting priorities, developing a work ethic, and persevering. This is a valuable book for every family library!"

Roger Staubach
NFL Hall of Fame Quarterback

"Chad is extremely dedicated and committed in his spiritual life. His family and professional life are equal testament to Chad's dedication to being a man of God on and off the field. I highly recommend *It Take Commitment* for every American youth."

Emmitt Smith
Dallas Cowboys, Running Back

COMMITMENT

IT TAKES

CHAD HENNINGS

MULTNOMAH
BOOKS

IT TAKES COMMITMENT
published by Multnomah Books
a part of the Questar publishing family

© 1996 by Chad Hennings

International Standard Book Number: 0-88070-991-X

Printed in the United States of America

Unless otherwise indicated, all Scripture references are
from the *Holy Bible: New International Version*, copyright 1973,
1978, 1984 by the International Bible Society.
Used by permission of Zondervan Bible Publishers.

96 97 98 99 00 01 02 03 — 10 9 8 7 6 5 4 3 2 1

To Tammy and Chase:
No commitment ever made was sweeter
than the one I made to you.

TABLE OF CONTENTS

ACKNOWLEDGMENTS

First, I want to give thanks to God for all the opportunities He has given me and for placing in my heart the drive to succeed. I give God all the credit and glory for whatever I've been able to accomplish.

God has truly blessed me with my wife, Tammy, and my son, Chase. They are my inspiration. Tammy's unconditional love and support help me keep my life in focus. We have been through a lot together—from separation to sickness—and throughout it all we have grown closer to each other and to God.

I would also like to thank my mother and father for the example they set for me. I learned early in life about commitment and the hard work and sacrifice it takes to stay committed to something. Thanks also to my "big" brother, Todd. You had more of an impact on my life than you probably know. Thanks as well to the rest of my family, whether siblings, grandparents, aunts, uncles, or cousins. Your support has been wonderful.

Aside from family, we are all profoundly influenced by other individuals whose paths cross our own. My high-school coaches, Reese Morgan and Jerry Eckenrod, are two men who taught me about dedication and discipline on the athletic field. Jerry Lewis, a military chaplain and true prayer warrior, taught me about dedication and discipline in the spiritual arena. These men have touched many lives and I thank God that I was blessed to be one of them.

Finally, thank you to the people at Questar for sharing a dream and helping that dream become reality. A special thanks to Blake Weber: You were always there with a word of inspiration and encouragement. Thanks also to Dave Branon and Tracy Sumner for listening and helping me to get my thoughts and words on paper.

It's amazing to realize that God has been with me from the beginning and He'll be there at the end. I can't thank Him enough for the commitment He showed us all by sending His Son to die on a cross for our sins. Thank you, Lord!

PREFACE

As a Christian and a father of a two-and-a-half-year-old, I've become concerned with the direction our society (and particularly our youth) has taken. When I read about six-year-olds murdering infants for no apparent reason and ten-year-olds throwing children out of high-rise windows because they won't steal candy for them, it pains me greatly. What have we done to ourselves? Where has the innocence gone?

Enough is enough.

I want to take advantage of the position God has put me in to try to influence young people for His good. Hard work and determination will help you go a long way in life, but think how much further you can go and how much more satisfaction you can get from life if Jesus Christ is your primary focus.

Of course, being committed to Christ is hard work. It's not easy to stay true to Him when all the temptations of the world—money, fame, sex, drugs, and so much else—are constantly forced on you by our society. I've flown jets in combat and I've played on three Super Bowl championship teams, but the effort it takes to remain committed to our Lord and Savior in the darkness of this world far surpasses any physical challenge I've faced.

My plea to you is simple: Stay committed. It doesn't matter who you are or where you're from. Be committed to Jesus Christ in every aspect of your life—school, athletics, family, community. By taking responsibility for your life, you would be surprised how you can influence those around you for good.

As we proceed through this book, I'll explain more of what dedicating yourself to Jesus Christ means. I'll tell you some stories about my life, stories that I hope will challenge you to sacrifice yourself for the Lord. I hope that through the events of my life you'll see that nothing worthwhile comes without effort. I'll introduce you to my hometown, where I first found out that if something's worth doing, it's worth following through with excellence. I'll introduce you to the Air Force Academy, where high demands were placed on me, demands that still help me succeed. I'll introduce you to my life in the military and my job of flying fighter aircraft, where there is little margin for error and no room for quitters. And I'll introduce you to playing professional football for the Dallas Cowboys, where it's a little like they say in basketball about the area around the basket: Don't bring no weak stuff in here!

At the end of each chapter, I've provided some "Workout Drill" questions to help you apply to your own life some of the things I've discussed. Use these questions to help you identify commitments you'd like to make and how you can fulfill those commitments each day.

I hope some of the important lessons I've learned will influence you to remain committed to the right things and, especially, to the right person: Jesus. And I pray that you will remember Christ's words to us, "I have told you these things, so that in me you might have peace. In this world you will have trouble. But take heart! I have overcome the world" (John 16:33).

NUMBER 95. TAKES HIS PLACE ON THE DEFENSIVE LINE FOR THE DALLAS COWBOYS.

THE SUPER BOWL

IT DOESN'T GET ANY BETTER THAN THIS

Nothing good comes in life or athletics unless a lot of hard work has preceded the effort. Only temporary success is achieved by taking shortcuts. Set goals and go after those goals with integrity, self-confidence, and a lot of hard work.

ROGER STAUBACH

To a professional football player, there's nothing like running onto the field at the Super Bowl. With tens of thousands of fans cheering (and hundreds of millions watching on television worldwide), your heart pounds and chills run through you. You've committed yourself to months of grueling conditioning, running drills, reviewing film, practicing and developing game plans, and playing every game with everything you have. Finally, that commitment pays off. You have a chance to win it all.

As a Dallas Cowboy since 1992, I've had the honor of playing in three Super Bowls. I've felt my heart pounding and my mind racing as I've run through the tunnel that connects the locker rooms to the field. I know the challenge of keeping my mind focused on the job at hand—winning the game—in the midst of the Super Bowl hype and the crowd's hysteria. And I've felt the fear of letting down my teammates and fans. After all, no football player wants John Madden to draw a circle around him on the telestrator for everyone to see his mistake.

On January 28, 1996, I ran through the tunnel at Sun Devil Stadium for Super Bowl XXX. For the third time in my professional football career, I felt the thrill as eighty thousand fans cheered, creating the roar that sends adrenaline coursing through your body.

But this time was different.

The thrill I felt that day dwarfed any I've felt before any other game, including my two previous Super Bowls. Why? Because this time two areas of my life to which I've committed myself converged to share a moment in time.

Right after we stood in respect for the national anthem and the flag, I heard a familiar rumbling sound, a sound that defines another chapter of my life—my years in the Air Force. I looked up to see a four-ship of F-16s conducting a low-level flyover, this time in the "missing man" formation to honor the crew of the Challenger, the space shuttle that exploded during takeoff ten years earlier. As a pilot, the sound of fighter jets touches a chord deep within me. That flyover evoked the sensations I felt every time I climbed into the cockpit of my aircraft and powered up the engines—excitement, power, and the nervousness that comes from putting myself on the line.

What made that flyover even more special was that some of my Air Force buddies were flying those jets. I get a chill down my spine just thinking about it.

That flyover really got my blood flowing. I was ready to play.

The Thrill of the Game

When you've made it to the Super Bowl, you want to do whatever you can within the rules to help your team win. You play your part, supporting your teammates all the way. After all, you've made it this far only because you've committed yourselves to working together toward the same goal.

In the third quarter of Super Bowl XXX, I had my chance to play a small part in one of the key plays of the day—Larry Brown's first interception.

We were ahead of the Steelers 13-7, and at the time Pittsburgh was moving the ball downfield. But we'd been putting pressure on them all day long, especially on quarterback Neil O'Donnell. We Dallas Cowboy defensive linemen pride ourselves on our abilities to rush the passer. If we know you have to throw the ball, we'll get to you. We just pin our ears back and go for it. We had committed to that goal as our defensive game plan, and we knew we could do it.

On this particular play, we were doing everything we could to get to O'Donnell. After the ball was snapped, I was the first one to get past my man when I sidestepped Dermontti Dawson, the Steelers' center. I was a split-second from sacking O'Donnell when he threw the ball, but I got my right hand on him as he released it.

Any time a defensive lineman can get in a quarterback's face as he throws the ball, good things will likely happen for the defense. This time was no exception. O'Donnell threw the ball right into defensive back Larry Brown's hands, almost as if Larry was the receiver O'Donnell had intended to hit. Larry rambled upfield with the ball and put us in scoring position. From there the offense took over, and when Emmitt Smith ran the ball in from the one-yard line, we were up 20-7.

As a defensive lineman, little things like putting pressure on the quarterback are important. Although you may not get the glory of intercepting a pass, you play your part to put your team in a winning position. That's how you fulfill your commitment to your team.

The play I made helped Larry Brown, one of my teammates, earn personal glory as he was later named Most Valuable Player of Super Bowl XXX. I was happy just to have had a hand in a key play like that.

I learned a long time ago that I didn't have to get credit for the big play in order to fulfill my commitment to my team. As a defensive tackle, I know that if I can flush the quarterback out of the pocket or cause him to hurry his throw, I am doing my job, even if someone else gets the credit for the big play. I'm content with that. After all, I have had the opportunity to do what any football player dreams of doing: contributing to success on a championship Super Bowl team.

Sack Happy

That pressure play wasn't the only time during Super Bowl XXX that I got to meet Mr. O'Donnell up close and personal. I also racked up two sacks during the game.

Let me stop here to explain how defensive linemen feel about sacking the quarterback. Sacks are our big plays, the plays we live for. To us, getting a sack is the equivalent of a running back scoring a touchdown or a quarter-back throwing a touchdown pass. And if you get a sack in the Super Bowl, you've hit the defensive lineman jackpot.

On my first sack during the Super Bowl, I had some help from my team-mates. On our previous offensive series, Leon Lett, Russell Maryland, and I were on the sideline talking about a certain line call the Steelers had made. We talked about what we would do the next time we heard that same line call. When we went out on the field, I was playing right defensive tackle, and it happened: The Steelers made the line call we had talked about.

I was ready. I said to myself, "Uh-huh, I know what you're going to do now!" I was able to use the knowledge I had gained from the earlier line call by hitting the gap quickly. I made an inside move, then took the left guard upfield and worked my way back toward the quarterback. O'Donnell rushed right into my arms, and I pushed him to the ground.

I had my Super Bowl sack!

Now, I didn't do a sack dance or anything showy—I don't believe in doing that kind of thing. But I did have a mini-celebration. I wanted to give the glory to God for allowing me to get this sack, so I put my hands together as if I were praying and pointed them toward the sky. It's a subtle acknowl-edgement, but it's my way of thanking God.

I wasn't trying to show off or draw attention to myself. That's not my way. I want to bring glory to God in everything I do, and this was no exception. I wanted to let people know that I'm a Christian and that I'm committed to thanking God for the good things He brings my way. It's just like when a receiver or a running back kneels in the end zone after making a touchdown.

A few people watching the game saw what I had done and mentioned it to me later. I think my wife was the first to notice. She was sitting in the stands and saw me do that. Later, she told me it brought tears of pride to her eyes.

God gave me another opportunity to thank Him—my second sack of O'Donnell in Super Bowl XXX. My first sack came from talking things over with my teammates and trying to outguess the Steelers. We had come to the field prepared, and that enabled me to get the sack. But my second sack was more like something out of touch football.

Once more we got pretty good pressure on the line. I was over the right guard this time. Our defensive end flushed O'Donnell out of the pocket, and as O'Donnell avoided him, he slipped and went down and I reached out and touched him. According to NFL rules, a player who falls to the ground on his own like that can get up and continue the play unless he is touched by a defensive player when he is down. Because I was the first defensive player to touch him after he went down, I got credit for the sack.

We call that a garbage sack and we laugh and joke and tease each other about it. But when I look back on it, it all looks the same on the statistics sheet. A sack is a sack. I look at it this way: I had to work hard to get back there to be the first one to touch him.

There was one more key defensive play in Super Bowl XXX that I helped execute. It wasn't a sack, but another kind of play we defensive linemen relish. It was a fourth-and-one play and the Steelers were going for the first down. They ran a straight play up the middle with Bam Morris, their 235-pound running back, carrying the ball. I came off the ball low, shucked my man, and met Bam head-on. I was the first one to hit him, man against man, shoulder pads against shoulder pads. I stood Bam up and the rest of my teammates joined in to finish the play. We had stopped the Steelers on downs.

At that point, momentum swung in our direction. The Steelers had been in our territory, threatening to score a touchdown or at least to get in field-goal position. They had momentum on their side. But they ran into a defense that was committed to doing what had to be done to achieve success. Meeting that type of opposition will take the heart out of any offense.

Commitment Has Its Rewards

I chose to begin this book by telling you about the Super Bowl because reaching that game is the ultimate goal of every player in the National

Football League. Play by play, game by game, commitment carries us toward that goal. We don't let anything get in the way. We keep our eyes set on the prize we've dedicated ourselves to winning.

Just to play football at the NFL level requires great commitment. But to compete and succeed at the Super Bowl level, as the Cowboys have year after year, requires a willingness to pay a steeper price and go that extra step. As Dallas Cowboys, we realize that everybody in the league is shooting for us. Whether it's in the preseason, the regular season, or in the playoffs, playing us is like the Super Bowl for a lot of teams. They are playing against the world-champion Cowboys and they want more than anything to beat us. We have to play our best all the time, because every team we meet is going to be fired up and eager to knock us off. We know we're not going to sneak up on anybody, so we have to be prepared physically and mentally.

Our commitment to stay on top in the National Football League requires that we dedicate ourselves nearly twelve months of the year. With the exception of a short break following the season, there really is no off-season for the Dallas Cowboys. We know that just being big, strong, and athletic isn't enough to reach the top (and stay there) in the NFL. It takes thousands of hours of hard work and discipline. In a word, it takes commitment!

Teams that lack that kind of commitment get lost by the wayside. You can see that as you compare successful programs with unsuccessful ones. The successful teams have high participation rates in off-season workouts. Players work out at their training complex in the spring and summer months, trying to get better. The unsuccessful teams are loaded with players who are off at home during the off-season, who don't take the time and effort to prepare themselves or build that cohesive bond that is so important for success at the NFL level.

One of the biggest sports stories of 1995 was about a team that reaped the rewards of commitment. Perhaps you read about the Northwestern University football team, which rose out of nowhere to win the Big 10 championship and earn a trip to the Rose Bowl. The Wildcats did that through commitment. While most college football players went home for the summer, a lot of the Northwestern players stayed and worked out together to prepare for the season. They developed that special bond, the attitude of "Hey, we're in this together! We can win! We're doing this as a team!" Never before had they done that, which is why Northwestern football had for many years been synonymous with mediocrity. But when the players made a commitment to themselves and to the team, they took their game to a whole new level.

That is the kind of commitment that my Cowboy teammates and I have to our team. We know this is what will keep us at the top of our profession.

I have to be committed to prepare physically for the season. My preparation for the season starts in March with weightlifting and running. I do these things because I know I have to be in good physical shape so that I am stronger, faster, and quicker than the guy I'm facing. I know I have to be ready and able to withstand six hundred pounds of human flesh coming at me on a double-block without getting blown out of the hole.

I also have to be committed to staying mentally ready for the season. I review videotape, study my opponents' line calls and their tendencies, even physically practice what they do so that when I see a certain formation—for instance, an offensive lineman setting up a certain way for a run block and another for a pass block—I have a mental edge. If I know what he's going to do, I know what I have to do.

A big reason commitment is vital for me during the NFL season is the sheer length of the season. Our 1995 schedule saw us play in five preseason games, sixteen regular season games, two playoff games (The Cowboys earned a bye in the first round of the playoffs) and a Super Bowl. That's twenty-four games, the equivalent of two college seasons. That can test any player's resolve! I know when the season starts that I'm in it for the long-haul. I can't be like a thoroughbred, able to run full-speed for short distances. Rather, I have to be like a quarter horse, which needs stamina for a longer race.

Without this kind of commitment, I wouldn't have had the opportunity to play for three Super Bowl championship teams. I didn't get the chance to play professional football after graduating from the Air Force Academy because I was committed to military service, but because I kept my commitment to continue working out, I was ready when the invitation came from the Cowboys. I know that if I had broken that commitment, I wouldn't have been ready when my opportunity came. The NFL would have slipped through my fingers.

Glorifying God in Your Commitment

It isn't easy to reach the level of success the Dallas Cowboys have enjoyed over the years. It takes a commitment to being the best we can be from game to game and from play to play. Without that level of commitment, we could never have achieved what we have.

But that kind of commitment is not reserved for football players alone. Any time we want to achieve excellence—whether it's in athletics, academics, music, relationships, or anything else—we have to dedicate ourselves to doing whatever it takes to reach those goals.

I believe this kind of commitment begins with a genuine commitment to Jesus Christ. Just as success on the football field depends on being dedicated to the weightroom, to good eating habits, to studying film and playbooks, and to the team concept, success in life depends on dedicating yourself to Jesus in everything you do.

Do you want to live an excellent life? If so, it takes commitment to Jesus Christ. This kind of commitment is essential, and it's modeled after His own example.

Look at how committed He was. He was committed all the way to the cross for us. That in itself says everything. He didn't go half way for us; He gave us all He had.

If we're to model ourselves after Him, we should be willing to commit ourselves to doing whatever we do for His glory. That means doing it the best we can. In all that we do—our spiritual lives, our family lives, our business lives, in our service to our country—our goal should be to approach life with the same kind of commitment Jesus had.

With God's help, I'm utilizing my talents to the fullest. God gave me athletic ability and a desire to compete in the athletic arena. Then He gave me the opportunity to play professional football for the Dallas Cowboys. I am therefore committed to being the best football player I can be so that I can bring glory to God.

That's what it's all about. And that's what I'm committed to doing.

WORKOUT DRILL

1. Although I'll probably never get a chance to play in the Super Bowl, I do have my own dreams. When I look down the road ten or fifteen years from now, what would I like to have accomplished?

2. What kinds of life commitments do I need to make if I intend to reach that goal?

3. What indicators do I have in my life that God might want me to go for that goal?

4. What obstacles might be in the way of my reaching my goal? How do I know the difference between a closed door that God has put there to make me change directions and an obstacle that He wants me to overcome?

5. If playing in the Super Bowl is one of Chad Hennings' biggest thrills, what would I say my biggest thrill would be?

A 4-H FAMILY FROM LEFT, GRANDPA, CHAD, HIS BROTHERS AND DAD.

STICK WITH IT!

No horse gets anywhere until he is harnessed. No steam or gas ever drives anything until it is confined. No Niagara is ever turned into light and power until it is tunneled. No life ever grows great until it is focused, dedicated, and disciplined.

ANONYMOUS

The road to any significant achievement in life is paved with commitment. I learned that priceless lesson as a small boy growing up on our family's Iowa farm, and it continues to shape my life today.

I know that I would not be where I am today without the kind of deep, unwavering commitment that enabled the Dallas Cowboys to achieve what they have over the past four years. But that commitment didn't sprout up in a vacuum. I am grateful to God for allowing me to grow up in an environment that taught me what commitment is. My parents, my brothers and sister, my high-school coaches, and many others instilled in me the importance of being committed not just to what I was doing, but to the people around me. Early on I saw what commitment meant and learned how to instill commitment in my own life.

Today I realize the value of commitment in every area of my life—commitment to God and what He wants from me, commitment to my family, and commitment to my position as a member of the Dallas Cowboys. And it all began at home.

A Piece of Americana

Keystone, Iowa, is not the kind of place you'd expect to find many National Football League prospects. Keystone covers about one square mile and is home to approximately five hundred people, give or take a hundred. Not much else is there, to tell you the truth . . . a grocery store, a bank, a service station, three grain elevators, the school—that's about it.

In its heyday—the '20s, '30s, and '40s—Keystone was bigger than it is today. At that time, Keystone was the hub of activity in the area. If anyone needed anything—food, farm supplies, entertainment, gas—they came to Keystone. But since then, people have found whatever they needed in the big city, Cedar Rapids. As a result of the competition, Keystone shrank.

What you find in Keystone these days is a lot of retired farmers. In fact, all of my grandparents retired from the farm and moved into Keystone to spend their golden years.

Although I consider Keystone my hometown, I didn't actually grow up in the city. The nine-hundred-acre Hennings farmstead sits about five miles outside of Keystone and about two miles from Elberon, an even smaller farming community. The house I grew up in has been in my family for more than 115 years. It dates back to the original Hennings who came from Germany and settled in what was then the western fringes of the United States. My great-great-great-grandfather was one of the first people who settled this part of Iowa, back in 1854. He and the other settlers came through New Orleans and traveled along the Mississippi River by boat to our part of Iowa. Great-great-great-grandpa Hennings built the Hennings farmhouse. Pictures now hang on the wall showing how the house originally looked. The family has added on some rooms over the last century, but it's basically the same structure.

An American flag waves proudly in the front yard, but it does not stand as high as our six grain silos. When the silos are filled, they hold 75,000 bushels of corn, which my dad and my brother Todd (who still run the farm together) use to feed the 4,000 head of feeder cattle that they tend each year.

I love that old house and the sounds and smells associated with it. Nothing takes me back to Iowa quicker than the smells of the cattle, the grain, the hay, and yes, even the manure. To me, those smells mean home.

I can still hear the sounds of the old homestead, too. I can hear my father getting up early in the morning and walking up to the door of my room. I can still hear him hollering, "Hey, you guys! Time to get up for school!" I can still hear the tractor engine turning over and the cattle mooing.

After my wife's first visit, she did admit she enjoyed the farm, but also admitted she couldn't quite appreciate those smells and sounds of the farm that I love. Although Tammy isn't a big-city girl, neither did she grow up on a farm, so she wasn't accustomed to the sounds and smells that were such a big part of my life. But for me, the cattle lowing at night is a lullaby—it's part of what I grew up with, a part of what I associate with home.

The Life of a Farm Kid

I still have a special place in my heart for the memories of my childhood. We didn't have the fast-paced lifestyle that the kids in the city did, but there was always plenty to do.

When my siblings and I were kids, we considered it a big treat to be allowed to ride our bikes into town. We thought nothing of riding the five miles to Keystone to play Little League baseball or visit friends or to go to the grocery store to get some candy. On Friday nights, Dad would play softball and we'd go to town with him to watch. Or if we didn't want to watch Dad play ball, we'd run all over town, play kick-the-can or softball, or do whatever else came to mind.

Other times, my brothers and I would roam around our homestead with our .22 caliber rifles, which we had since we were twelve years old. Handling guns was part of our education as farm kids, and Dad made sure we knew how to use them safely. We'd shoot tin cans and at rabbits, squirrels, raccoons, skunks, and anything else we could find. We had plenty of room to shoot and not many people to worry about hitting.

All these experiences—the sights, sounds, and smells—were part of my small-town upbringing. It was a great life. Today, when I talk with kids about my childhood, they often say, "Well, what did you *do*? It sounds boring." But I was never bored. To me, that kind of life was fun and invigorating. We farmers knew how to create fun for ourselves without relying on computer games or videos.

I wish my son Chase could have some of the same experiences I had growing up on the farm. I have to live close to the Cowboys' workout facility, so Tammy, Chase, and I must live in the metropolitan Dallas area. City life doesn't offer the same opportunities for children that small-town life does. I regret that Chase won't have the joy of getting up early in the morning before school to feed the 4-H calves. I regret that he won't learn the discipline of helping out at harvest time after athletics or have the opportunity to drive a tractor out in the fields. There are so many advantages to growing up on a farm that Chase will miss.

Lessons From the Farm

If there's anything that life on the farm will teach you, it's the value of commitment. Not only do you need commitment to do the things it takes to make a farm profitable, you need commitment to trust God during the hard times that are sure to come.

You have to trust God and learn to rest in His timing and His faithful provision. You have no choice but to leave your well-being in His hands day by day. All you can do is put your crops in and pray that God will provide.

Living with that and seeing what my parents went through each day— and now, seeing my father and my oldest brother Todd working on the farm—reminds me how strong our faith and character had to be in order to survive.

I just don't see how someone who's not a Christian can make it on the farm. The truth is, some don't. For example, a neighbor recently passed away. He was semiretired, still living and working on the farm. But Iowa got so much rain this year that many farmers couldn't get their crops in. Our neighbor died from a heart attack, probably from stress.

I'm sure my dad has stress, too, but he knows where to take it. To this day my father still talks about praying for peace of mind and security to make it day to day on the farm. God was a huge factor in my family. We always went to church, after-school classes, and vacation Bible school. We didn't have Bible studies in my house, but there were always prayers at night.

I'm so grateful to have grown up in an environment where God was so important. I can see now how it laid a solid foundation for things that were to come in my life.

A Lesson in Commitment

Participating in 4-H taught me several important lessons about commitment. You probably don't expect to hear the values of 4-H extolled by a guy who makes a living chasing down Barry Sanders and Brett Favre, but my experiences in raising cattle for 4-H have helped me succeed in other areas of life (*especially* in chasing down those guys!).

Involvement in 4-H is something of a cultural experience in the Iowa farmlands. Nearly all the kids around my home participated in 4-H. My mom and dad had, and all my cousins and close friends were involved in it, too. It was the thing to do.

I took seriously my 4-H involvement and viewed each project as tremendously important. When I was about twelve years old, my brother Todd and I worked on a project together. We had to care for and halter-break a couple of steers. The memory of Todd and me trying to halter break a 650- to 700-pound steer still makes me laugh. We were a couple of 130 pound kids, and those steers tossed us around like feed bags! But we had so much fun, and the experience toughened us. We knew we had a job to do, and we did whatever it took to succeed.

We also had to feed our steers in the morning and at night. When the weather got nice, we had to prepare them for showing season by walking them around our farm to condition them. Before any showings, we had to groom, clip, and comb our steers. Caring for a steer takes a lot of daily effort, but it pays off. One year my brother won Grand Champion, and one year I was in the finals!

Our parents let us know that it was our job to complete our 4-H projects, but they were always there to help us. They'd say, "Son, it's your responsibility," but they knew they had a big part to play. They understood that a ten- or eleven-year-old boy can take some responsibility, but that he'd need some help from Mom and Dad. A lot of times we would feed our steers in the morning or night, but there were often times when we couldn't feed the calves, so my dad would do it for us.

Taking on a 4-H project requires a pretty big commitment on the part of a young boy or girl. You have to feed your calf, halter-break, groom and wash it, and you have to clip its hair (my dad did the clipping because we were too young to handle the shears). And when you take the steer to the fair for competition, it's a four- or five-day event, so you have to be there constantly from six in the morning until late at night.

Working with a steer is just another example of how my brother and I learned that when you start something, you don't quit. Tending those steers could get a little old, but we received great rewards when we persevered. When you sell a thirteen hundred-pound steer for nearly a dollar a pound, as Todd did, you realize the value of sticking with a project!

I think my dad really enjoyed our time in 4-H. He seemed to have a lot of fun passing on to us some of the things he had learned about farming. And one of the biggest lessons he learned, of course, was about commitment.

A Father's Commitment

I couldn't talk about the value of commitment without talking about the man who lived it for me every day as I was growing up: my father. My dad taught me, by his actions and his words, what commitment really is.

Despite all my fond memories of growing up on the farm, I now realize that my dad didn't have an easy life as a farmer. He worked hard to provide for our family. He faithfully ran that farm every day. My brothers and I helped him, but my father bore the burden of making it profitable. Most of the time, he didn't mind. Farming was his passion and still is.

Dad would buy market beef—three thousand 750- to 800-pound calves—and feed them until each weighed 1,200 to 1,300 pounds. Then he'd sell the cattle to a packing plant. That's how he provided for us.

While simply buying, feeding, and selling animals may not sound too difficult, it takes true commitment to run a cattle farm. There is no time off. A farmer can't take a day off. If you're sick or need a break, no one substitutes for you. You have to figure out ways to get the chores done. The animals have to be fed twice a day. And not only do you have to feed the animals, you have to grow the food they eat such as corn, alfalfa, and soybeans. It is hard work.

But running a farm isn't tough just because of the hard work. It's also difficult because of the unknown. You can't control all the variables: the weather, the government, the market, crop disease, mechanical breakdowns. If you could control any one of those variables, farming would be much easier.

Can you imagine not knowing from day to day what's going to happen to your livelihood, not being able to control any one variable in your job? As a National Football League player, I can control numerous variables on my job. I can control how much I work out and how much I prepare for the games. If I'm hurt I can sit out yet still get paid. But as a farmer, any number of uncontrollable events can financially ruin you overnight.

Farming is an up-and-down business, and my dad has paid the price of riding that roller coaster. For example, the early '80s were tough. Back then, many farmers had to file bankruptcy before the banks could foreclose on their homes and land. High interest rates, too much debt, and the structure of government programs squeezed many family farmers out of business.

I watched as my father wrestled with the decisions he had to make in order to outlast the tough times. To help our family and our farming business survive, he made the tough choice to sell some land that had been in our family for a long time, just to finance the debt from the lean years.

At the time, I didn't understand why we had to sell that piece of property, which had been in our family for quite a while. I wondered why there wasn't something else we could do. But now I can see that selling the property was probably the best thing Dad could have done; some of my friends' fathers were forced to declare bankruptcy. I was probably in my midteens when I started to understand a little more about finances, about my father's struggle with all the stress of having to restructure. Only then did I understand how fortunate we were not to have to declare bankruptcy.

Sure, my father felt the pressure. Sometimes he broke down, wondering if we were going to make it. I saw him cry, fearing for the welfare of his family. I imagine that, although he had his family around him, he felt very lonely bearing the burden of providing for us during the lean times. I've always considered my father a strong man, and I still do. He's the strong foundation for the family I grew up in. So when I watched this strong man break down, I felt the stress, too. I was humbled by how much my father took on his shoulders for my family, for me.

My father has weathered some rough times as a farmer. But no matter how tough things got, no matter how much pressure he felt, my father never gave up. Instead, he gathered his resources and created ways for us to survive. For example, my dad always kept meticulous financial records, carefully tracking his expenses and income. When finances started tightening up and other farmers had to look for work elsewhere, my father gathered his accounting records, took them to his bank, and showed the bankers that his farm was a profitable operation and that it was worth their time and effort to help him restructure his finances so he could ride out the crunch.

My father's actions during those lean times spoke volumes to me about commitment. Through his choices, my dad showed me that making something work requires you to go through the valleys as well as the peaks. He showed me that when you start something, you don't quit—no matter how tough things get. His example forever instilled in me the value of commitment.

A Loving Father

My dad was the John Wayne, the stalwart, of the family. He was the cornerstone of our household, as a father should be. He taught me the value of commitment and hard work. He convinced me that anything worth doing is worth doing with all my strength. He showed me what it means to be a man.

And he loved me.

There are a thousand things about my dad that I try to emulate for my own son Chase. My father is the type of man who would do anything for the people he loved. To this day, he's always there any time I call. Ever since I can remember, I have always felt comfortable talking to my dad about any-thing—any problems or any questions I ever had.

Best of all, perhaps, my father is a man who isn't afraid to let his emo-tions show. When I saw him break down over the farm's financial prob-lems, it wasn't the first time I had seen him cry. The first time I saw tears roll down my father's face became one of the most emotional moments I've experienced.

My little brother Kent had injured his foot in an accident. I was on our riding mower when Kent caught his foot under it. The whirling blades broke all his toes and took a chunk out of his foot. I picked him up, carried him into the house, and we rushed him to the hospital.

At first, the doctors didn't know if Kent would fully recover. There was nerve damage, and we didn't know if he would ever walk normally again. That was when I saw my father cry. He was so distraught over my little brother's injuries that he wept.

As it turned out, Kent stayed in the hospital for just four days and he recovered fully. But that experience changed the way I looked at my father. I loved my dad, and seeing him cry added a new dimension to our rela-tionship. I felt closer to him. I thought, *Man, he's human and he has emo-tions.* I had always looked up to this man as a rock—yet he let his family see him cry. I had seen a wonderful side of my dad, an event for which I'll always be grateful.

One of the things I appreciate most about Dad is that he always sup-ported me in whatever I did without trying to sway my decisions. He didn't push me in any certain direction. He didn't say, "You're going to join the Air Force," or "You're going to go out for football." Those were my decisions to make, and he allowed me to make them.

My dad allowed me to make decisions, but he also taught me *how* to make them. He taught me about taking all the variables, weighing them, and then making up my mind. I am so grateful to him for that.

Dad was incredibly supportive of me in whatever I chose to do. From the time I wrestled in the kids' tournaments through my high-school career, I can remember him being there in the stands, cheering me on. When I'd win, he'd be there to celebrate with me. When I lost, he'd say, "OK, you know why you got beat." Then he'd tell me what he saw and say, "Let's do it next time."

Whenever I needed encouragement, Dad would give it to me. For instance, when I was in high school, I would work all day long baling hay before I could work out. Sometimes I finished working in the fields late and I'd be tired. But he'd always give me a little nudge and say, "You've got time to go work out."

To this day, Dad supports what I'm doing. He comes to three or four of my games each season. He'd like to come to more, but he can't get away from the farm that often.

I'm happy to say that my dad hasn't changed a bit since I left home. My brother Todd lives close to Mom and Dad on one of our adjacent farms. Todd and his wife have two boys and a girl, and my father interacts with his grandchildren the same way he interacted with his children.

I can look at Todd's kids and know that they'll have a chance to learn about commitment. And so the cycle continues.

Gridirons, Grapplers, Guitars—and Mom

My mom is a remarkable woman. She deserves so much credit for instilling in me many of the mental aspects of personal commitment. She exemplified commitment in her own life and I drank in the lessons she lived out for me and my siblings.

Here's something that tells you clearly the kind of woman my mother is: The year I graduated from high school, my mom graduated from college. Even today I cannot fathom how she accomplished that feat! She would wake up at 5:30 A.M., make sure Dad and all her kids had their breakfast, get us off to school, then travel thirty-five miles to the University of Northern Iowa in Cedar Falls to take classes all day long. Then she'd drive home, make dinner, and take time to study for tests and work on her papers. When she had finished her schoolwork, she'd spend the rest of the evening doing all of her work for the church, her community service, and working for other organizations she had volunteered for. Not only did she do that every day, but she still made it to many of our athletic events to cheer for us.

At the time that Mom was working on her degree, raising us, and helping run the farm, my brothers, my sister, and I didn't think twice about it. We never knew anything different. But now I realize what a phenomenal woman she is. I can see how her drive and commitment helped us when we were growing up. She was the glue that held our family together. My mom is a perfect example of commitment.

Yet even in the midst of all her activity, my mom paid attention to the details of raising her children to be well-rounded adults. It was very important to her that each of us develop some sort of musical ability or talent. And through her desire to bring culture into my life, I learned another valuable lesson in commitment.

When I was about six years old, Mom asked me what musical instrument I would like to play, and without hesitation, I said just one word: guitar. So guitar it was. My cultural development would include lessons in plucking the guitar. But once the lessons began, they seemed to go on and on and on. And although I did learn to play the guitar, I was once again exposed to that familiar motto: "Once you start something, you never quit." It was one of my dad's favorite sayings, and my mom fully supported it.

I enjoyed playing the guitar for about three years. I liked being able to play music (if that's what you can call what I played during the first year). But after that it got a little old. I decided I'd rather be playing outside with my friends than inside practicing my guitar. Also, I was beginning to take a more active role in helping my father on the farm. I didn't want to sit down in the house for a half-hour or forty-five minutes every day and practice the guitar when there was so much to do outside. I didn't have the discipline to play that instrument well, but because I had started something, I had to keep going.

I remember telling my mom I didn't want to play the guitar any more. I should have guessed what she'd say: "This is something that you're going to appreciate later on down the road. I want to make sure all my kids have some sort of musical background."

So, under the rule of commitment that governed our household, I kept playing the guitar. I took lessons for about six years, but for three or four of those years I wished I didn't have to.

Today I see that my mother's wisdom was right on. I still have the guitar. I don't have the time to practice much, but I can still pick up the guitar and play all the notes and all the chords. I appreciate the fact that Mom made me keep my commitment.

I had a similar experience with the drums. While I was still playing the guitar, I thought playing the drums for the elementary-school band would be pretty neat. After about two weeks, however, I realized the drums weren't for me. Once again, I didn't want to practice, to do what it would take to excel. But once again, Mom said, "Hey, you started this, and you're going to follow through and finish it for at least the school year."

So that's what I did, even though I wanted to do other things in school. Had it been up to me, I probably would have lasted two weeks. Somehow I forgot that I was a Hennings, and a Hennings had to finish what he or she started. Mom meant it when she said, "You're going to follow through on this." I'm glad I did stick with it, because, once again, I learned a lot. Aside from learning the value of commitment, I learned an appreciation for music that continues to this day.

I will always be grateful to my parents for making me keep my commitments. While they encouraged me to try many things, they also insisted that I not hop from thing to thing; I learned to stick with it and be committed to it, to give it an honest shot. That's what I'll do with my son. I'll encourage him to try many things, but to stick with each one and give each one an honest chance before he shoots it down. I won't force him to stick with it when it's not right for him—I learned that from Mom—but I want him to give the things he tries a fair chance.

So you can see where I learned commitment. It was our family's password!

The Call of Sports

Because of my size and physical skills, I was much better suited for sports than music. In Iowa, two sports are almost the birthright of every kid: wrestling and football. Iowa has some of the best high-school and college wrestling programs in the nation; in fact, it's the number one state in the country for wrestling. In addition, Iowa schools have always been known for their excellence in football.

And I competed in both football and wrestling . . . except for my fateful sophomore year, a time I want to tell you about.

When I was a sophomore at Benton Community High School, located in a nearby town called Van Horn, I faced a real crisis. If you play or have ever participated in athletics, you've probably come face to face with this type of problem.

I decided not to go out for wrestling. I always loved participating in football, but I was tired of wrestling. I had wrestled on the junior-varsity level as a freshman, but when wrestling rolled around the following year, I was scared to go out. I was afraid I would fail, afraid of losing, afraid of the apprehension that hits you in your stomach right before a match, afraid of having to lose weight to get down to the appropriate weight class. (That was about 140 pounds ago when I wrestled at about 145 to 150 pounds.)

Understand that wrestlers are some of the most dedicated athletes around, if not *the* most dedicated. They have to cut weight and maintain that weight during the season. That can be a horrendous experience for some wrestlers. I myself loathed having to lose ten or twelve pounds to make weight. At the time I didn't know enough about nutrition and how to lose weight properly. When you starve yourself a couple days before a meet and you don't drink enough liquids—all so you can make weight—it's hard on the body.

Wrestling was also scary for me because it is one-on-one. Even though it's a team sport in the sense that you earn points for your team, it basically comes down to you going mano a mano, you versus the other guy. I'd always get so nervous. If you've ever wrestled competitively, you know what it's like. Unlike football, in wrestling you have no one else to rely on but yourself. When you step onto the mat, you're out there alone.

As a freshman, that pressure was almost too much for me. I got so nervous before every match that it was hard for me to get out there and compete. So when I contemplated another season of that nervousness, another season of starving myself to lose weight, I decided I just couldn't face it.

Because I could talk to my dad about anything, I told him that I didn't want to go out for wrestling. He was very supportive and offered a suggestion. He encouraged me to try something different that winter. He had played basketball in high school, so he suggested, "Well, if you don't like wrestling that much, maybe you should give basketball a shot."

Dad didn't tell me to stick with wrestling if I didn't want to. To him, commitment meant if you started the year on the wrestling team, you finished the year on the wrestling team. He told me, "If wrestling is not your thing, you don't have to continue to do it, because that's not smart, either. But if you commit to the year, you're committed for the year."

In my dad's eyes, trying out for basketball didn't make me a quitter. I had completed my freshman year, and each new year was a new opportunity to branch out and acquire different interests and skills. He never opposed us trying new things. But if I had started the season in basketball, then wanted to switch to wrestling in the middle of the year, he would have pressed me to complete my commitment to the basketball team. In this situation, however, he fully supported my decision.

So that winter, I refused to face up to my fears. Even though I really liked wrestling, I let my fears get in the way. When wrestling season started, I wasn't on the mat.

That was a hard decision for me, and once I made it, life didn't get much easier. The wrestling coach, Jerry Eckenrod, was one of my favorites, and I felt I was letting him down. To make the situation even more complicated, Coach was the father of my best friend in high school, Grant Eckenrod. Even though I saw Coach a lot before the wrestling season because I spent so much time with Grant, I never said anything to Mr. Eckenrod about my fears or told him ahead of time that I wouldn't be a part of the wrestling team—even though I knew he was counting on me. I didn't want to face his disappointment and disapproval. Most of all, I didn't want him to talk me out of my decision.

Eventually, I talked to Coach Eckenrod about my decision. He seemed very understanding, even sympathetic as I explained my decision to him. I felt some relief after I had talked to him, but there was still that knot in the bottom of my stomach. I felt that Coach was disappointed, even though he realized it was ultimately my decision to make and he respected it.

That winter I went out for basketball. I started on the sophomore team and we had a pretty good squad. But even though I enjoyed myself that season, I felt something was missing. All along, despite how well basketball went, I knew I should have been wrestling. I believed I let myself down by not rising to the challenge. For me, that was the worst part of the situation. I knew I should have been out there wrestling, but I took the easy road. I copped out.

When basketball season ended, I spent a lot of time thinking about my decision. In that time of soul-searching, I realized that I was meant to be a wrestler. I had the natural physical abilities to succeed at the sport, and despite my fears during my sophomore year, I really had the mentality to face an opponent one-on-one and win. I decided that I'd return to wrestling the next year.

I can't say I enjoyed the process of not following through on a commitment, but I learned some valuable lessons from the experience. First, I learned that you can never be successful if you fail to face your fears. I had opted out of wrestling for two reasons: I hated to cut weight, and I didn't like the anxiety of going head-to-head against my opponent in front of large crowds. Well, when I decided to put away the hoop dreams and wrestle again as a junior, those two situations were still there to challenge me. Running from my fears would never make them go away. Only when I faced my fears could I conquer them.

Second, I learned that all rules need to be applied with a measure of grace. Though my parents believed that once you started something you followed it through to completion, they allowed me to explore other interests. I can still hear my father's words, "You can do whatever you want to do, but once you start something, you never quit. You stay committed to that."

Even though I wish I had remained committed to wrestling my sophomore year—I could have learned a lot from living out that commitment—yet choosing not to wrestle that season may have been the right decision in terms of the long-range outlook of my sports career. I grew a lot physically that year. I gained about twenty-five pounds, and I grew three or four inches taller. Had I been forced to cut weight to wrestle in a certain weight class, I might have stunted my growth.

If I had it to do all over again, I wouldn't skip wrestling my sophomore year. But even so I learned some valuable lessons. The biggest one is this: God uses all situations for good, even when we make mistakes.

Back on the Mat Again

At the end of my sophomore year I made a personal commitment to Coach Eckenrod—and to myself. I said, "Coach, I made a mistake. I'll be back next year."

Coach was happy to have me back. He knew that when I came back the following year I'd be committed to giving everything I had to be the best wrestler I could be.

When wrestling season rolled around my junior year, I vowed that I would never let my fears rule me again. And they didn't! In my junior season I wrestled so well that I qualified for the state tournament. By my senior year, I had reached a weight of 215 pounds and was wrestling heavyweight. That year, I won the Iowa state heavyweight championship!

Winning the state wrestling championship is definitely the highlight of my entire high-school sports career. I feel that way, not only because of the victory and the emotions that come with it, but because of the contrast between my sophomore year, when I failed to face my fears, and my last two years, when I faced my fears and overcame them. Knowing that I had conquered what had once held me back made that state championship so much sweeter!

You want to know how I did it? By commitment. I committed myself to training, to working out extra hard, and to paying the price off the mat. I went from being a kid who was afraid to wrestle to a young man who became a state champion. To do that I had to put everything I had into practices, lifting weights, and running. I had to get myself in optimum physical shape. I also had to get prepared mentally. I had to think through my strategy, how I'd handle victory and, more importantly, defeat. I had to decide that maintaining strict discipline and standing on my own to face an opponent meant more to me than racking up wins. If I was going to commit myself to wrestling again, I was going to do it for the long haul.

I gained so much by making that choice. Yes, the state championship was an incredible highlight of my life, something I'll always cherish. But the lessons I learned about commitment were even more valuable; I continue to apply them every day of my life. That whole experience chiseled and hardened the way I approached athletics and my ability to focus. It helped me add a whole new dimension to the way I trained. I'd go home my junior and senior year after practices and visualize all the moves I had to make on the mat. I'd visualize single-leg takedowns and other wrestling moves. Once I decided to tackle my weaknesses and even exploit them to make myself a better wrestler, I never had to worry about my commitment to that sport again.

I've spent a lot of time telling you about my wrestling experiences in high-school, and you might be surprised because you probably thought I would talk more about football. And I will. But I must say that the lessons I learned from wrestling—including the decisions to take a season off and then to return to the sport—were foundational in helping me succeed in football at the Air Force Academy and with the Cowboys. Wrestling taught me the value of commitment to excellence, a commitment that goes beyond personal comfort and safety, a commitment that makes you want to put yourself on the line for worthwhile results.

Once more, my parents were primarily responsible for helping me learn these lessons about commitment. Many people fear failure and so avoid trying new things. My parents' view was, "If you fail, fine; but you don't quit.

You try, and you work as hard as you can to make yourself better." They made going back to wrestling so much easier for me. And because of their encouragement and acceptance, I did succeed.

Yet even though my parents taught me this valuable lesson, I have to admit I'm still afraid to fail. I'm still nervous about being the center of everyone's attention and falling short of success. But now I know how to handle that fear, and I know how hard I have to work to be successful. Fear might never go away, but it can be mastered. That's the challenge.

Todd the Taskmaster

My parents weren't the only ones in my family to challenge me to strive to be the best I can be in everything I do. My brother Todd, who is sixteen months older than I am, is the one I credit the most for getting me on the road to good work habits in football.

Todd was a great example to me. Dedicated to excellence in football, he practiced constantly and did whatever it took to become the best football player he could be. In high school, Todd played quarterback. When I started out, I played tight end and occasionally quarterback. Because we played complementary positions, Todd and I constantly threw the football back and forth. And I mean *constantly*. Whenever we had free time, we threw that football.

And I hated it.

I hated it because in my mind Todd was *making* me do it, and sometimes I didn't feel like catching his passes over and over and over again. I didn't feel like running patterns for him. I grew tired of all the repetition—I wanted to do something else.

But as time went on and we continued to practice, I began to see improvement in myself. I noticed that my techniques were getting better. I was seeing success—hard-won, valuable success.

But throwing that pigskin back and forth wasn't the only evidence of Todd being a maniacal taskmaster. No, he went one step further. He took me to all the off-season, summer workouts. We'd work out together in the sweltering heat—and my brother never missed a practice. We'd sweat, we'd drink gallons of water, we'd practically pass out, but we wouldn't miss practice. Those summer practices weren't mandatory with the coach, but they were with Todd. We worked hard and we saw results.

Todd started at quarterback his senior year and I moved up to varsity and played tight end. All of those nasty patterns we had run under the hot Iowa sun paid off. For the first time since my brother and I had started playing organized football, we were on the same team.

It was fantastic to play on the same team as Todd. Sometimes he'd lay the ball up over the middle to me, just as we had practiced. Of course, I'd get clobbered by a linebacker or defensive back, as tight ends often do. But the "punishment" was worth being on the receiving end of Todd's passes. All those hours of throwing the ball back and forth paid off in our games.

Todd was a good influence in other ways. We weren't just workout partners and teammates—we were competitors. We had a huge sibling rivalry, a rivalry that carried into nearly all areas of our lives. At suppertime, put the food on the table after the blessing, and watch out! We would race to see who could get to the mashed potatoes first.

Separated by sixteen months in age and two years in grade, we were always trying to outdo each other. It was a big-time rivalry, and it could get stressful. I always tried to outdo him because I was always compared to him. He was older and I wanted to show him and everyone else that I was just as good as he was in everything. Todd got good grades, so I had to get better grades. Todd did well in sports, so I had to do better in sports. He was a huge motivation for me.

Sometimes we'd go on long-distance runs that Todd thought were such good ideas. Now, the land in Iowa is laid out in square sections one mile long and one mile wide. Todd and I would run around one section every day, a four-mile route. And it didn't matter what the weather was. Sweltering heat or drenching rain, Todd would say, "Time for our run, Chad. Let's go!" They were tough runs, and to help us tolerate them, we turned them into competitions. All along the route we'd try to run ahead of each other.

Todd knew exactly how to motivate me to improve. Even though I may not have wanted to work out—maybe I had a little lazy tendency back then—he had a way of getting me going. He knew how to push my buttons. He'd say things like, "You're not going to get any better" or "You can't do that." And I always responded with the attitude, "Well, I'll show you!" I think I truly respected Todd in what he did, and seeing his success as a football player convinced me that his tough workout regimen was the right thing to do.

My brother and I also competed against each other in the "Punt, Pass, and Kick" competitions in our area. We were in different age groups, of course, but we still competed to see who could throw or kick the football farther. Todd was really good. One year he went all the way to the districts, which is one step away from the championship. I thoroughly enjoyed competing with him, and I held my own against him, too. Todd was always the better passer, but I was the better kicker.

We maintained this competition and discipline through high-school, and though I sometimes doubted Todd's sanity (and mine for following him), I never doubted the results. Working out with Todd showed me the importance of an off-season workout regimen.

Inevitably, the competitive nature of our relationship led to fights. Most of the time, these "fights" amounted to nothing more than spirited wrestling matches, but one time we got into a real fight. It happened at the end of my sophomore year in high-school, right after Todd had graduated. He was giving me a hard time and we got into an argument. One thing led to another and BAM! I hit him! Before we knew it, we were going at it furiously. In two or three minutes we grew dead tired, and both of us bent down with our hands on our knees to rest. It's funny to remember now, but the conversation during our rest went something like this: "How are you?" "I'm OK." "You need a rest?" "Yeah." "You ready to go?" And then we went back at it.

I remember the fight so well because it was the first time I got the better of Todd. Finally, all those years of pent-up frustration at competing with him were released. Neither of us got badly hurt, and we still laugh about our little fight today.

There was something missing the next two years after my brother graduated and went off to college. He was my training partner, my quarterback, my brother, and my friend. With him gone, I felt a tangible void. But what remained was the value of commitment, the value of hard work and sticking to a task despite the obstacles. Those are lessons that I will always cherish.

Todd taught me that commitment didn't mean just showing up on game day. He taught me about commitment not by his words alone, but by his actions. He showed me the preparation it takes to be in peak condition for the season.

Despite all our competition, Todd and I had (and still have) a deep love for one another. A real closeness existed between us, and we always looked out for each other. We might fight between ourselves, but neither of us would have allowed someone else to mess with the other (although that never happened). It's like the old saying—brothers fight like cats and dogs, but if you mess with one, you've messed with every one of them.

Today, Todd is still my best friend, and I still appreciate what he did for me in those early days. He knew what he was doing all along, even though I didn't appreciate it at the time. It took me a couple of years to realize that he was doing me a great service. I'm sure he had a dual reason for pushing me so hard. For one, he probably saw me as a training partner, yet he also knew that I'd get better as he got better. And today I remember his example and maintain the discipline he exhibited when I prepare myself for each professional football season.

Coached to Commitment

Two other people in my life greatly influenced me to be a committed athlete when I was in high-school and I still admire their strength of character today: my football coach, Reese Morgan, and my wrestling coach, Jerry Eckenrod.

Morgan and Eckenrod were caring men who went beyond the call of duty to help their athletes train in the off-season so they could excel during the season. These two coaches motivated all their students, and Todd and I were not exceptions. They encouraged Todd and me to pay the price, to do the weightlifting and running that would prepare us for football and wrestling.

Because of their commitment to us, I really admired Morgan and Eckenrod. I wanted to be like them.

All during the summer, Coach Morgan would be at the school lifting weights with us, mentally motivating us, taking time out of his personal schedule to be with us. I can still hear him encouraging us: "One more rep! One more rep!" And Coach Morgan is the type of guy who you could call any time, day or night, under any conditions. If you needed him, he'd be there (even after you graduated from high-school. I'll tell you about that in the next chapter).

Coach Eckenrod also stood by me, even when I thought I had let him down by not wrestling during my sophomore year. He welcomed me back my junior year and invested his time and expertise in helping me hone my wrestling skills. His investment led to the success I enjoyed, including the state championship.

Football on My Own

After my brother graduated from high-school, my football experience changed drastically. We had a mediocre team my junior and senior years, winning only half of our games in both seasons. I felt frustrated because I wanted to succeed. My teammates had a lot of talent, but we just couldn't put together winning seasons. As our team struggled, I had to call on the mental strength that my family had instilled in me.

On the personal side, I enjoyed some successes. I made all-state as a punter and kicker my senior year and second-team honorable mention as a tight end. But team success was so much more important to me.

I found it's hard to rely on teammates coming through for you. In wrestling, I could win all by myself. I knew that if I put in the training and the effort, I didn't have to depend on anyone else; it was me against my opponent. But football is much different. Through our struggles, I learned that football is a team sport and that if you're going to win, you're going to have to motivate the other players on your team. That means getting them in the weightroom in the off-season. That means being an example of good behavior and encouraging them to do the same instead of drinking, doing drugs, or getting in trouble with the law.

I had seen that commitment in my brother, that dedication to excellence not only in himself but in me. And I had learned the value of commitment from my parents. So I felt frustrated when I saw so many guys just going through the motions. I depended on them, and they weren't physically or mentally prepared. It showed when the season got underway.

Despite the disappointment of failing to get into the state playoffs (Todd got there when he was a junior), my senior year brought individual success through the honors I received in football and wrestling. The honors were wonderful, but even more important to me was fulfilling that burning desire within myself to do my best in whatever I tried.

In my senior year, my classmates voted me "Most Likely To Succeed." Yet while I felt honored that other students viewed me that way, such an honor is no guarantee of future excellence. Many students who gain a similar honor fall by the wayside, tripped up by lack of desire, or sinful practices, or poor friends. I had no way of knowing whether some of these things might cause me to stumble in the years ahead, but I did have something that I knew would help me: the mental recording of my dad's voice constantly playing in my head, "Once you start something, you never quit."

It's a good thing. I was headed for the Air Force Academy, and if there's one thing that's hard to quit, it's the military.

WORKOUT DRILL

1. What fears do I struggle with as I try to succeed in my areas of interest? Is it better for me to avoid them and not try to conquer them, or should I gut it out until I succeed?

2. Who are some people who motivate me? Are there others who would motivate me if I would listen to them and their instruction?

3. What pearls of wisdom have I learned from my parents—good advice that they tell me over and over but that I sometimes try to ignore?

4. What activity am I forced to do (like Chad's workouts with Todd or his guitar lessons) that I can't stand? Have I ever sat down and thought about the advantages of this activity compared with the disadvantages?

5. Nobody knows whether commitment to something will pay dividends as it did for Chad. What are some other benefits to sticking to a task, even if it doesn't lead to a career or success?

CHAD TAKES PART IN A SPECIAL CEREMONY PRIOR TO THE JAPAN BOWL. A COLLEGE ALL-STAR GAME.

CHAPTER THREE

THE AIR FORCE ACADEMY

WHEN I SIGNED MY LIFE AWAY

The greatest reward for a man's toil is not what he gets for it,
but what he becomes of it.

JOHN RUSKIN

When we were kids, my brothers and I sometimes thought we had it pretty rough on the farm. We loved our home, but it was a lot of hard work. We had to feed the cattle, help with the crops, bale hay, clean out the cattle sheds. There was always something to be done.

But I didn't know how tough things could be until I went to the Air Force Academy.

Do This, Do That

The Air Force Academy presented me with the first major culture shock I ever faced (the second one was leaving the Air Force to join the Cowboys). The first thing they do is break everybody down so that individuals disappear and a team is born.

When our fourthclassmen class (the equivalent of the freshman class of civilian universities) arrived on campus at the Academy just north of Colorado Springs, our commanding officers didn't give us much time to get used to our new environment. They let us know right away that summer vacation was over and they meant business.

On the day we arrived, our commanding officers gathered us together, shaved our heads, and let us know in loud, no-nonsense terms that none of us was an individual any longer. We were part of the team.

I found it was an impressive team to be on. Out of several thousand applications, only a thousand to fourteen hundred people can be accepted each year. So the Air Force must be extremely selective in who it accepts. You must have a 3.65 or better grade-point average and a high SAT score just to be considered. So everybody in basic training is basically just like you. They're the valedictorians, the state champion wrestlers, the all-state or all-American football players. And you're thrown into the mix with all of them.

Basic training at the Air Force Academy is different from the typical enlisted or ROTC basic training. We had to learn the basics such as how to march, the rifle manual, and survival techniques. We had to memorize *Contrails*, a book containing page after page of quotes from military leaders, politicians, and other notable people. For the next year, this book would be our constant companion. Not only did our commanding officers demand that we read this book, they ordered that we memorize it word-for-word. We had to know that book inside and out, because whenever a higher-ranking cadet felt like quizzing us about it, he or she could do so. Any of them could interrupt anything we were doing and ask us to quote from that book.

Life at the academy follows a strict regimen developed by the military to prepare cadets to defend our country. Every morning we got up at 6 A.M. There are no snooze buttons at the Air Force Academy. When it's time to rise, you get up or else.

In the first hour of the day, besides wiping the sleep out of our eyes, getting dressed, cleaning our area, and making our beds, we had to memorize a menu of the day's meals, read a newspaper to keep up on current events, and get out our *Contrails* book to review the assigned quotations for the week and brush up on the ones we'd learned in previous weeks.

We did all that preparation for the benefit of the upperclassmen. It was our job to wake them up and get them prepared for the day. As with everything else at the academy, we had a strict procedure for waking the upperclassmen. We would say something like this: "It's 7:06. The menu for the morning meal is as follows . . ." then list the breakfast items for the day.

After the upperclassmen showered and dressed, they'd come to where we fourthclassmen were assembled and quiz us on anything they wanted to, such as the day's current event, assigned quotes from *Contrails*, or the menu for the noontime or evening meals.

And we had to be ready to answer any question they'd ask.

As first-year Academy students, we had to eat "square meals," and I don't mean eating food from the four basic food groups. We had to eat our meals standing at attention, squared off to our plates. As we ate, we had to stand looking directly at the Air Force Academy insignia at the top of our plates. We could look at that insignia and nothing else.

While we ate in that position, the upperclassmen would ask us to quote passages from our book of quotations. As we ate, some upperclassmen would actually sit there, wait for us to put food in our mouths, and then ask us questions before we were done chewing. We had to be ready to answer at any time, so we learned to take small bites and chew fast.

In addition to those regimentations, we had to take part in morning jogs, outdoor training sessions, military marching drills, rifle lessons, pushups and situps, and physical-fitness tests. All this was required *in addition* to classroom work and, in my case, the hours I had to put in for football.

You know what stands out in my memory about that first year at the academy? The blisters I got from having to jog in combat boots during basic training. As I was one of the tallest guys in the class, they always stuck me farthest up in the formation and to the right. The shortest people were to the left and behind. As I tried to keep time, I had to run with all my weight up on my toes because of the blisters on my feet. Eventually, I had to go to the medics and have them treat my blisters. The medics would pop them, put salve on them, and wrap them up so they wouldn't get infected.

Then there was the cramping. I sweat a lot, and if I don't keep a lot of fluids in my body, I cramp pretty easily. I had a problem at times with cramping during basic training. On top of that, the summer of my basic training was unusually hot, so it was a real challenge for me. It was a real test of my commitment, having to run two miles or whatever with blisters and with my hamstrings locking up.

On the more pleasant side of my first-year academy experience, I can say that I formed some special relationships with some of the people who went through it with me. There's something about going through a trying, challenging experience with other people that will draw you close to them. We've all heard it said that people who have survived cancer or endured some sort of accident, catastrophe, or wartime experience form a special bond with one another. I can say from experience that it is definitely true.

I don't tell you these details so that you'll feel sorry for me, and I'm not complaining about the rigors of academy life. Instead, I mention all this to reinforce my strong conviction that anything worthwhile is worth working for.

Before I attended my first class at the academy, I knew the kinds of expectations placed upon me by the upperclassmen and the Air Force. Knowing those expectations, I made a commitment to the Air Force; and because of that commitment, I pursued excellence in meeting all the demands those upperclassmen made on me.

Why the Air Force?

You may wonder why I chose to go to the Air Force Academy if I knew in advance how tough it would be. After all, I could have chosen a school where the coaches and students would treat me specially simply because I played football. I could have attended a college where it was up to me how I chose to spend my time. But, as crazy as it may sound, I chose to attend the Air Force Academy precisely *because* I knew it would be difficult.

There's a great example of that attitude in American history. In the early 1960s, President John F. Kennedy stood before the American people and told them that the United States would be the first country to put a man on the moon. He promised that the U.S. would do so before the end of the decade. In that speech, he said, "We choose to go to the moon, not because it is easy, but because it is hard." And on July 20, 1969—when I was just three years old—Neil Armstrong stepped out of the lunar module Eagle and put his foot down on the dusty surface of the Sea of Tranquility. America had succeeded at something very, very difficult, and we all stood proud on that day.

I like that kind of spirit. I, too, choose to do things not because they are easy but because they are difficult. I don't particularly enjoy adversity in and of itself, but I do enjoy the fruit of hard work. My family succeeded on our farm by having that mentality. It's how my brother taught me to succeed in sports. And I had the feeling that attending a tough school like the Academy would help me succeed in life.

The idea of attending the Air Force Academy first began to interest me when I was a junior in high school. Although everyone in my family was a big Iowa Hawkeye fan and the idea of attending that university in Iowa City somewhat appealed to me, I really wanted to attend school out-of-state. I wanted the adventure of traveling and seeing the world. And the Air Force Academy promised those kinds of opportunities.

Not only did academy life provide some of the adventure I wanted, it also gave me the opportunity to experience the discipline and challenge of the military lifestyle and to obtain a first-rate education in the process. Not knowing what I wanted to major in, the well-rounded, balanced academy education seemed like a good option for me.

A Coach's Dedication

I knew I wanted to attend the Air Force Academy, but merely having that desire doesn't get you there. To be accepted as a cadet takes just as much commitment and determination as the Air Force expects of you once you're actually in. And I couldn't have achieved that goal without the help of a man I've mentioned before—a coach I admire greatly, Reese Morgan.

I first talked to Coach Morgan about going to the Air Force Academy during my junior year in high school, which is when you start the college-application process. I was at a junior wrestling meet for the elementary kids, running one of the scorer's tables, and Coach sat down and said, "Have you thought about where you'd like to go to college to play football?" Without hesitation, I said, "I've thought a lot about the Air Force Academy." I didn't realize it at that moment, but our conversation planted a seed in his mind.

I had seen the campus when our family had taken a skiing vacation in the Colorado mountains, and I was impressed with the campus' beauty. I learned the academy had the balanced education I was looking for, and I also knew that its football program was on the rise. It seemed like the more I looked into it, the more I wanted to go. It was all so appealing.

I really wanted to play college football, but I had a problem. No school had highly recruited me. Sure, I got some feelers from Iowa, Iowa State, Purdue, and Minnesota, but apparently no one was too impressed with a kid who played for a small, rural high-school team that won only half its games. It didn't seem to matter that I was 6' 4" and weighed 220 pounds. It didn't seem to impress anyone that I could punt, kick, and play tight end *and* defensive positions. And it didn't seem to make any difference that I was so dedicated to off-the-field training that sometimes Coach Morgan had to come to school at night and throw me out of the weightroom.

Still, I had been learning a valuable lesson by this point in my life: Be committed, and if you remain committed, you can never go wrong. Even if you gain no rewards beyond the satisfaction of doing your best and never giving up, you've gained reward enough. Most often, though, the commitment will go beyond the reward of personal satisfaction to result in something good happening to you.

And if the Air Force Academy understood anything at all, it was commitment.

That's why I cannot be grateful enough for what Coach Morgan did for me. After I told him I was interested in the Air Force Academy, he took action. He did something almost unheard of in the annals of coaching (although for a man of Coach Morgan's character, it wasn't that unusual).

Coach Morgan became my one-man Chad Hennings public-relations staff, whose singular goal was to get me into the Air Force Academy to play football.

In the spring of my senior year, Coach Morgan collected some highlight videotapes of our games, put them in his car, and drove from Iowa to Colorado Springs to talk to the Air Force Academy football coaches. Imagine! He drove eight hundred miles one way to tell the Air Force coaching staff about this big farm kid back in Iowa.

When Coach Morgan arrived in the foothills of the Rocky Mountains, the first person on the academy coaching staff he encountered was a graduate assistant. No doubt part of this graduate assistant's job was to shoo away people like Reese Morgan. But when Coach Morgan asked the graduate assistant if he would look over the tapes, he reluctantly agreed. The graduate assistant watched the tapes and became impressed enough with what he saw that he showed the tapes to another coach, who was equally impressed. Soon the coaching staff was asking Morgan some questions.

I found out later that when Coach Morgan delivered that tape to the academy, the Air Force Falcons had just one recruitment slot left. I know now that if Coach hadn't made the special effort to introduce the Air Force coaching staff to me, I probably wouldn't have received that last slot. I will always be grateful to Reese Morgan because of his commitment to me. That commitment and his take-charge attitude are the main reasons I had the privilege of playing football at the Air Force Academy.

A Test of Commitment

Even though Air Force coach Fisher DeBerry and his staff were interested in me coming to the academy, I didn't sail through their recruiting procedures without facing some obstacles. The coaching staff wanted to meet me that winter, but I was smack in the middle of my senior season in wrestling. I had a commitment to fulfill to myself and to my team. I had my sights set on the state championship. And because the big wrestling tournaments took place on the weekends, I had no immediate opportunities to go to Colorado Springs to meet with the football staff.

I had a big decision to make, one I knew could affect the rest of my life. I really struggled with that decision. I had to ask myself, "Do I shirk a previous commitment to pursue an important goal, or do I risk my future football prospects and an incredible education experience to maintain my dedication to something I've already started?" Ringing in my ears was my parents' training that told me that I had started something and I couldn't look back. And yet . . . if I didn't meet with the Air Force coaching staff, they might think I wasn't interested in playing for them or that I wasn't willing to make sacrifices to fulfill their recruiting requirements.

I chose to fulfill my wrestling commitments and I found, once again, that commitment has its rewards. The academy coaching staff saw my decision as evidence of dedication, a character quality they value. Those coaches liked the fact that I didn't want to take a recruitment trip at the expense of my wrestling commitment, so they waited until after the wrestling season to meet me. They reserved a spot at the academy and on the football team until our meeting.

I made the right decision, both in terms of my commitment to wrestling and to my future at the Air Force. As I look back on this key decision in my life, I see it as another way God has taught me to stick to my guns and receive His reward. God honors commitment!

Getting to the Academy

Eventually I took my recruiting trip to the academy and I saw firsthand everything it had to offer. I had seen the academy from a distance and been intrigued by it, but when I got an up-close look, I fell in love with it and with the area.

Colorado Springs and the Air Force Academy are snuggled in the foothills of the Rocky Mountains. After living in the Iowa plains where you see nothing but flat land for miles and miles, those mountains overwhelmed me! Imagine waking up every day and looking out your window at those majestic mountains. How could anyone resist?

(And little did I know that Colorado was also the home of a beautiful girl named Tammy. But to tell you about her now would be getting ahead of the story.)

My recruiting trip succeeded in just about every way. I got a chance to watch as the Air Force football team was going through a spring practice and I talked to the coaching staff and learned all about the football program. Then I went to dinner with one of the players. I also went through academic counseling, where I talked with an instructor who showed me the curriculum. It was pretty much an in-and-out sort of thing—one day and one night, and the next morning I was gone. But I really was impressed. The recruiting trip solidified my desire to attend the Air Force Academy. I knew that it was the place for me. Not only did I fall in love with the Rocky Mountains and the campus—an eighteen thousand-acre slice of heaven on the front range of the mountains—I realized that the Academy offered what I wanted academically.

I returned to Keystone, knowing that the Academy football staff wanted me to play for the Air Force Falcons. Yet that wasn't enough to get me in; I still had to earn a place at the Academy itself. I had to jump through all the hoops to show the Air Force that I belonged there.

The first thing the Academy wanted to know was my grade-point average. I had achieved a 3.85 and was in the top five of my class of 120. But even though my good grades helped, I still had to cut through all the red tape that every Air Force Academy recruit faces. I had to undergo a series of interviews and a variety of physical examinations. On top of that, I had to fill out the paper work necessary for obtaining a nomination to the Academy from a congressman.

Reaping the Rewards of Commitment

In high school I dedicated myself to both athletics and academics. I was always a straight-line kind of guy, and I worked hard at both. And though I may have missed some of the "fun" my friends had, I received the reward for my commitment when I applied at the Academy. After going through all the required tests and paperwork, I received an appointment to the Air Force Academy. It made me feel great to know that while I had to apply just like everyone else, I could have gained admission on my own merits, regardless of whether I played football.

I was in, and now it was time for me to get ready for what was ahead.

I've always downplayed the positive things that happen to me, and my appointment to the Academy was no exception. Downplaying things is how I try to remain humble. If I get an accolade, I usually respond by saying, "Well, that's very nice. Thank you." I try to maintain an even keel and go on my merry way. I never get too excited and I never get too depressed. I think that kind of attitude helps in the long run. I know it helped during the process of being accepted to the Academy.

Once I obtained an official acceptance, I had time to slow down and think about the future. There was no way of knowing what the future had in store for me, an eighteen-year-old kid about to leave home for the first time—and, as it turned out, for good. Except for short visits, I never lived on the farm again.

Even though I tried to handle this new challenge in my usual way, I started to get nervous about going. Downplay it as I might, and as prepared as everyone had tried to make me, I was troubled by the unknown. I didn't know what to expect from basic training. I worried about whether I'd succeed in football. And then there were all those college classes I'd have to take. I didn't know whether I could get the good grades needed to stay at the Academy. So as I headed for Colorado, I left with a lot of questions weighing on my mind.

My future was unsure, and I endured the same self-doubts that every young person feels when heading off to college for the first time. But I knew what was behind me. I had parents who taught me the value of hard work and sticking to a task, siblings and friends who supported me all the time and pushed me when they needed to, and coaches who cared for me almost as if I were their son. These people had prepared me well. Now it was up to me to carry the ball from there.

No Time to Worry

One of the good things about the way we started off at the Academy is that if I had any questions when I arrived, they didn't matter. I had no time to think about them. It was a big-time culture shock to have every minute of every day planned. We fourthclassmen had all we could do just to remember the things that were required of us, let alone have a few contemplative moments to think about whether we liked being there.

The contemplative moments we did enjoy, although rare, usually came while attending services in the awe-inspiring, picturesque chapel on the Air

Force Academy campus. You may have seen pictures of this silver building whose pointed roofline draws the viewer's attention upward toward the heavens and God. I remember attending one of those chapel services and staring at the beautiful, stained-glass windows that overlook the Academy. In that calm moment of reflection, I said to myself, "This is tough. Really tough. But I'm going to make it." I felt completely at peace.

Despite the difficulties of surviving that first year, I knew the Academy was where God wanted me to be. Although I had not yet committed my life totally to Him by this time, I could sense that He had guided me to the Academy. The consciousness that God cared for me was another truth my parents had instilled in me. My dad would respond to tough times by saying, "It's in God's hands. We don't have any control over it." We lived our lives with an understanding of God's goodness. That perspective helped me whenever I needed assurance that I would succeed.

I made it through that first year as an Air Force Academy cadet. And I survived college football, which I'll talk about a little later. But instead of throwing a party to celebrate our toughness and our intelligence, the Academy sent us on an end-of-the-year field trip that I'll never forget.

How I Spent My Summer Vacation

Traditionally, fourthclassmen take a trip at the end of the school year. But this trip is not a time to bring the camera, shades, and a tape player for a cushy week on the beach. It is survival camp called SERE (Survival, Escape, Resistance and Evasion training). It turned out to be just as rough as it sounds.

SERE camp was a three-week course that all fourthclassmen were "invited" to attend. And guess what—everybody went, all twelve hundred of us. The Air Force took this trip seriously because its pilots had to know how to survive if they were ever downed behind enemy lines.

We spent the first week in instructional classes, learning how to take care of ourselves in the wild. We studied books and listened to lectures about survival. Our instructors taught us many survival skills, such as how to tie different knots and how to evade the enemy. They taught us what plants we could eat, which berries to pick, how to set snares and traps, how to skin a rabbit or other small animal, how to build lean-tos and so forth. We learned everything you'd learn as a Boy Scout, and much more.

After the instructors filled our heads with knowledge, we headed for the mountains and forests for five days. During the first few days, our instructors showed us how to set up tents. We learned to build a tent using only a poncho or anything else we had on our backs. Next they taught us to camouflage our tent with brush.

Then came the really good part. We were ready to put into practice what we had learned during the first days of survival training. It was time either to sink or swim in the wilderness.

Alone.

For the next couple of days, each of us was on his own. We would try to sleep during the day so that at night we could practice our navigation skills. We would attempt to get from point A to point B, a kilometer to a kilometer-and-a-half apart. All this time, others hunted us, as if they were enemy soldiers. Our job was to find a partisan camp where we could take refuge. We spent a lot of time hiding and evading and navigating by the light of the Colorado moon.

Each of us was given a compass, a knife, a blanket, and a poncho. That's it. This trip took place in June, an unpredictable time of year for weather in the Rockies. Sometimes it snowed, other times we had to duck from lightning. We even endured a hailstorm one night.

But the weather wasn't the only obstacle nature had for us. There were the ant bites. And the starvation. Each day our instructors gave each of us a hard roll and a cup of soup, and that was all we had to eat for that day. Of course, we could eat anything else we could scrounge up, such as berries or bugs, but there wasn't much left after twelve hundred trainees had foraged for a week.

After the survival segment, we spent the next four days in a simulated prisoner-of-war camp. While there, we learned about the various interrogation techniques that enemies might use if they captured us. We learned how to give away certain "information" without endangering our country's cause, how to play dumb, and how to resist the enemy in that environment.

Trainers were allowed to do certain physical things to us to teach us about the torture we might endure in a real POW camp. They'd put a cadet in a little box and lock him up to simulate isolation. They'd make him spend up to a day-and-a-half in a little cubicle where he'd have a cup in which to go to the bathroom and a 6 x 6 inch board with a 2 x 4 nailed on top of it to sit on, although they never wanted to see him sitting down. If our instructors opened our cubicles and caught us sitting down, they could take us out, do whatever they wanted to us within reason, and throw us back in.

If you were in that kind of scenario, most of the time they would get you in a safe physical restraint hold, such as wrapping a towel around your collar and tightening it up and jerking your head back and forth. Or they'd cram you in a little 3 x 3 "penalty box." They had little torture devices where claustrophobic cadets would go nuts. They were playing mind games—simulated, of course. Nothing physically threatening.

A lot of people in charge of these camps really got into the role-playing. They seemed to enjoy being "the enemy." When you go through survival training, you're supposed to throw yourself into role-playing. You realize that the situation is simulated, but it is very realistic. I know there were times I was afraid. They brief you on what can happen, but you still don't know how long it's going to last or what exactly will be done to you. That's part of the mind game. It's not intended to be a game; it's deadly earnest.

All this training sounds pretty gruesome, but it had a genuine, worthwhile purpose. Our instructors wanted to teach us important survival skills. If we ever went into combat, we had to be ready to face the worst possible circumstances. We had to be mentally tough so that we could handle whatever might happen to us. We had to realize that if we became prisoners of war, we wouldn't have the option to quit.

Not too long ago, Americans saw how valuable that kind of training can be. When Air Force pilot Scott O'Grady was shot down behind enemy lines in Eastern Europe, he had no choice but to live off the land and depend on his wits until he was rescued. After O'Grady returned home safely, he credited his survival training with helping him make it. He had endured the same kinds of conditions we had gone through during our end-of-the-year excursion into the Rockies.

So, as strange as it may seem, that difficult summer was one of the highlights of my Academy experience. It was a pain going through it, but it was a great experience. It stretched me as a person and showed me again what a committed person can do. And it instilled in me some intensely valuable lessons in flexibility. Instead of nudging me away from my commitment to this tough educational system, it bound me to it even more.

Becoming a Human Again

It's hard to explain the kind of relief it was to get my freshman year at the Academy behind me. The only thing I had to compare it to at the time was the emotion I felt when I first beat Todd. It was something like that, only taken out another order of magnitude.

When you finish your first year at the Academy, you become a person again, an individual. You get your identity back. No longer are you a "Doolie," as they call the freshmen. No longer do you have to worry about an upperclassman dressing you down without so much as a moment's notice. You don't have to worry about having someone walk up to you and say, "Give me JFK's quote from 1962," or "Let's drop and do twenty." You can walk anywhere on the campus and you don't have to be at attention during mealtime. (Incidentally, the policy concerning meals for fourthclassmen has been changed. Now they let the freshmen eat in peace. No longer do they train them at the dining tables).

Finally, it's your turn to give the first-year cadets a hard time! At least, that how many second-year cadets feel.

As a second-year cadet or thirdclassman, I too could decide to treat the fourthclassmen the same way I was treated. Some people seem to enjoy doing just that. But I never did. I know how tough your first year is without having people treat you so miserably. I remember waking up every day and saying, "Why am I here? Why do I subject myself to this?" I did what was essential as an upperclassman, but I didn't join in many of the indignities the other cadets inflicted on the freshmen. I didn't want to flaunt my power over the first-year people. The way I see it everyone deserves a measure of respect. Besides, the new fourthclassmen weren't the ones who had treated me that way, so giving them a hard time didn't make much sense to me.

It was nice being an upperclassman, but it presented me with a big decision.

A Chance to Get Out

When I signed on to attend the Academy, I committed to a four-year hitch followed by several more years in the service. I knew that if I wanted to receive the benefits of a free education at one of the top institutions in the country, I had to give something in return. That's what you call a commitment.

But the folks at the Air Force Academy realize high-school seniors don't always know what they're in for when they sign on. Therefore, the Academy provides a window of opportunity for students to opt out of their commitment after two years. (This is the reason why some people jokingly call the Academy the best junior college in the country.) Many students choose to leave the program at this time. Other second-year students choose a "stop loss" program where they can attend civilian schools for a year, collect their thoughts, and then return. This option provides students a second chance to think about their commitment.

As I looked at my own situation after my sophomore year, I also had some second thoughts. Once I visited some friends who attended Arizona State University. While there I stopped by the football field to watch spring drills. As I saw what life "on the outside" was like, I wrestled with my commitment. If I stayed at the Academy, I'd be in the Air Force for at least the next seven years—and more if I wanted to be a pilot.

I did a lot of soul-searching then. I talked with my dad, and as usual, he didn't tell me what to do. He simply asked me, "What do you want to do?"

I told him I wanted to be a pilot. Obviously, I was in the best spot to make that dream come true. I also prayed and talked with other people.

I spent a lot of time thinking about my decision. I weighed the benefits of staying or leaving. In the end, I decided that my friends were at the Academy, that I felt almost at home there, that I loved the area, and that I was getting an incredible education. Also, I had enjoyed a great sophomore football season and had a lot of things to look forward to.

I decided to stay.

I knew that my decision to stay effectively killed any chance for me to play professional football. But at that stage in my career, I didn't really view myself as a pro-caliber player, so I didn't think I was giving up that much. Yet I felt I was saying good-bye to a dream. It was tough to give up that dream, because in my heart I wanted an opportunity to play professional football and prove what I could do. It was a difficult thing for me to accept. Although I wanted the opportunity to play football in the NFL, I knew I would be a long shot. It's tough for a college All-American to make it in the first place, but it has proven that much tougher for players from the Academy.

You have to understand that the Air Force Academy is not considered a conduit to the NFL. We aren't talking about Notre Dame or Michigan. In fact, at the time only two other Air Force graduates had ever been drafted by the NFL. Ernie Jennings, a 1968 graduate, was chosen but never played in the league. More recently, Steve Russ was picked by Denver but is serving a military commitment that will keep him out of the NFL until after the turn of the century.

When I went through my time of soul-searching, I knew that if I stayed at the Academy, I'd probably play only two more years of football and that would be it. But then I'd have my education and I'd have the opportunity to fly jets, which is one of the reasons I had come to Colorado Springs in the first place. I saw a path for myself and I felt content with it. I had made the right decision.

But in addition to all the great experience I was gaining, I had come to the Academy to play football. And while I was there, I was going to do that with everything within me.

Falcon Football

I played tight end my freshman year of football with the Air Force. But because we played a wishbone offense and ran the ball most of the time, not many passes came my way. In fact, I didn't play much.

In a wishbone offense, the tight end is basically an extra blocking lineman. I was a reserve during my freshman season and we didn't run too many two-tight-end formations. So I got in the game only when we were in goalline or short-yardage situations or if we were far ahead. I got in maybe five or six plays a game. It was difficult for me to accept, but I tried to remain patient and continued working hard.

We finished the regular season 7-4 that year and were invited to play in the 1984 Independence Bowl in Shreveport, Louisiana. My mom and dad came down to see the game, but I got in the game for only one down. There was never a need for a second tight end in that game.

I was disappointed, of course, but I was also motivated. I decided then and there that things were going to be different the following season. I was going to be playing. I hadn't come to the Air Force Academy to be satisfied with being on the team; I wanted to contribute on the field. When I talked to Dad later, I said, "I'm never going to let this happen again. I'm here to play football and I'm going to do whatever it takes to get on the field." He patted me on the back and said, "You know what to do."

Like never before I dedicated myself to getting ready for the next season. I made a commitment to myself that I was going to do whatever I had to in order to get a chance to play.

Then, in the spring of my fourthclassmen year, the coaching staff switched me from tight end to defensive tackle. They told me in spring football they wanted me to start the following season, so naturally I agreed with the switch. At the time, I was small for a Division I defensive tackle. I weighed about 240 pounds, and a good-sized defensive tackle in college runs about 270 or more. But the coaches began to teach me how to play the new position.

I had to overcome some adversity as I was getting ready for my sophomore season. In the first half of spring practice, just before spring break, I severely injured my ankle. I didn't have enough time to sufficiently rest before beginning the second half of spring practice when I was supposed to be learning this new position. My sore ankle severely limited my mobility, and that made it tough to learn the position with any confidence.

I got through spring practice and I did well enough in the fall to keep my starting spot. But I really didn't know how I would do when I actually had to play defensive tackle in a game.

I well remember my first start as a Division I football player. A football player's first start at any level is always a major milestone, a rite of passage. My first start in high school was like that; it was the same thing with my first start in a Division I game. It was a thrill to play in front of thousands of fans. In high school, the biggest crowd I ever played before was fifteen hundren to two thousand fans, tops. So to play in front of fifty thousand people at Falcon Stadium was an incredible moment for me. What made it even more special was that my parents were there.

Yet it was also a tough day for me. Before the game, I was so nervous that I paced back and forth on the sideline to try to calm myself down. I was able to relax enough to play, but by halftime I was dead tired. I had expended so much nervous energy pacing back and forth before the game that the football staff almost had to wheel me off the field. In the second half, I could barely get off the bench to play.

My defensive coordinator, Bruce Johnson, had a way of pushing my buttons, just like Todd had in high school. That's how he motivated me: He chewed me out. He walked up to me and barked, "You can't even get up to play." And I said, "I can do the job."

I had to work extra hard that next week not just to save face, but because I felt as if I were on the bubble. I knew there was another guy on the team who could start. I knew that if I didn't do well, I could lose my starting position, and I wouldn't allow that to happen.

My first game taught me something very important about playing football, especially at the college level. I had to make some changes in how I dealt with my nervous energy. I was wasting a lot of it prior to getting on the field. I hadn't learned to control it, so I set out to change my way of thinking before a game. I learned to control that energy, to harness it. And I did just that for the next game. I had learned my lesson.

Look Who's (Almost) No. 1!!

That year, our team finished with a 12-1 record. We won our first ten games and many sportswriters conjectured that Air Force could become the top-ranked team in the country. One newspaper, *The New York Times*, had rated us first on the basis of its computer rankings.

But then we went to Provo, Utah, for our showdown with Brigham Young University. At halftime, we were ahead 21-7 and appeared to have the game in hand. But we failed to stop BYU quarterback Robbie Bosco in the second half and we lost 28-21. By losing that game, we surrendered the chance to play in a projected national championship game in the Fiesta Bowl against Penn State.

Still, we had the honor of playing in a bowl game that year against the University of Texas at the Bluebonnet Bowl. We defeated the Longhorns 24-16 to give us the 12-1 record for the season.

As it turned out, my switch from tight end to defensive tackle was a great move for me. I was named to the Sophomore All-America Team and was second-team All-Western Athletic Conference.

My sophomore season was also memorable because of what we were able to accomplish as a team. We were out sized by everybody we played. But what we lacked in size we possessed in discipline. My teammates and I were always well-conditioned, strong, and able to handle our own against anybody. We had a plaque in our locker room that reminded us that the falcon kills prey larger than itself. That's what the Air Force Falcons did every week. It was another example to me of what commitment can do. We may have been smaller than our opponents, but the commitment we had to be our best made the difference.

Back to Earth

Our football team wasn't so successful in 1986, my junior year. We lost several players to graduation, including Bart Weiss, our fine quarterback, and we had a lot of injuries during the course of the season. We finished 6-5 and didn't go to a bowl. It was a very disappointing year for me and my teammates. But we remained committed, did our best in every game, and tried to set ourselves up for an excellent season in 1987.

But the benefits of our junior-year dedication didn't come easily. In spring practice, two of my best friends suffered major knee injuries. I remember pulling everybody on the team together after those injuries to talk it over. I almost broke down as I said, "We've got to stay committed. We've got to stay focused and pull together."

I had anticipated that the year ahead would be the last that my classmates and I would play football. I had high hopes that our senior football season would be great, and I didn't want to see anyone give up because of adversity. I wanted to encourage us all to remain committed to our goals.

Throughout my last year, a group of seniors would get together before each game at one of our hotel rooms. We'd talk about what we'd do to win each game. The seniors were a close group, and we did our best to fulfill our leadership role for the team. Because of the adversity we faced in spring practice, we had bonded together to create an atmosphere of excelling under pressure. We carried that mind-set into our senior year and put together a successful season. That happened only because we were all committed to the same goal—excellence.

Our commitment paid off, because in my senior year everything started clicking. We finished second in the Western Athletic Conference (again, we lost to BYU) and went on to play Arizona State in the Freedom Bowl, where we lost to the Sun Devils.

I sprained my medial collateral ligament (MCL) during my last regular-season game when I was chopblocked. It was the first time I'd ever been seriously injured in a football game. I had only three weeks to get ready for ASU, but I was going to play; I had a commitment to my teammates. I had to overcome a lot of pain, but I did what I needed to. I ended up getting a couple of sacks and was named the Freedom Bowl Most Valuable Player.

Say Hello to the NFL?

In my last year of Falcon football, something happened inside me. For the first time in my college football career, I began to honestly think that I might be good enough to play in the NFL. Of course, I knew that my dream to play in the NFL was out of the question because of my long-term commitment to the Air Force. But things began to occur that I had never expected.

First, I was voted the Western Athletic Conference Defensive Player of the Year and I was chosen as an All-American. Then I won an award that really woke me up to the possibility of playing pro ball: I received the Outland Trophy, an honor given each year to the interior lineman voted the best in the country.

This just doesn't happen to guys who play for the Air Force. We're the players nobody else wants; we're the athletes who have signed our lives away to the military. How cruel to tease us with such awards which will surely be followed by men in suits offering professional football contracts. It's cruel because we've already signed on the dotted line of a different document. We're committed to the Air Force, and we're not available.

When the NFL draft rolled around in April 1988, I watched the first day of picks on ESPN between my afternoon classes. I wasn't chosen, which didn't surprise me because of my commitment to the military. But I hoped, just a little, that I'd be surprised by a team wanting me to play for them. But it didn't happen.

By the second day of the draft, I didn't even want to watch. I felt disheartened. I went to classes, then worked out in our weightroom, blowing off some steam. As I was pumping iron, someone came in and gave me the news: The Cowboys had chosen me in the eleventh round! Right away, a news reporter arrived to interview me about being drafted.

I knew the Cowboys had been interested in me. They had kept in touch throughout some post-season collegiate games such as the Japan Bowl and the East/West Shrine game, and I had talked several times with Gil Brandt, their player-personnel director at the time. He always made a point to say, "If the opportunity comes, we'd like to have you." So I had an inkling that the Cowboys might draft me.

The strange thing is that although the Cowboys had drafted me, they never called to tell me. I guess when a player goes in the eleventh round, he doesn't get a phone call. Besides, it seemed like a token draft pick. The Cowboys were simply taking a small chance.

But still, I felt great! I considered it a trophy to add to my other football honors for the year. For the rest of my life, even though I couldn't actually play pro ball, I could say I had been drafted. I'd be able to tell my grandkids about it some day. I imagined telling them, "I never had the opportunity to play because I was in the Air Force, but I was drafted, and somebody thought I was good enough to play."

Still, getting drafted was a bittersweet experience. Although I felt exhilarated, I also felt frustrated. In fact, that time was one of the most difficult of my life.

I had spent the previous eight years of my life lifting weights in the off-season, training hard for football, while continuing my education. All of a sudden, BANG! It's over, or at least postponed for eight years until I had fulfilled my military commitment. I was so disappointed. I really wanted to play.

Yet today I can honestly say that having to wait to play pro ball was the best thing that could have happened for my football career. First, I wasn't physically mature enough to withstand the rigors of professional football. I weighed only 250 to 255 pounds. Second, I wasn't mentally mature enough as a young college kid. I didn't have the emotional stamina for the preseason and a full season of professional football. Last and most importantly, I was not spiritually ready. I believed in Jesus Christ, but I wasn't mature enough in my Christian faith to be able to stand for Him in the spiritually challenging circumstances that the NFL brings.

Temptations are thrown at NFL players day in and day out—the women, the drugs and alcohol, the opportunity to cheat (such as using steroids). All kinds of temptations and evils are out there. It's tough enough to be a rookie in the NFL, but it's even harder to turn away from those other things if you don't have the spiritual foundation. Without that, you're like a lamb among wolves. I don't know if I would have succumbed, but I do know that I was not spiritually ready to play in the NFL.

I signed a contract with the Cowboys and they gave me a small signing bonus. Already, I was further ahead in the game than I had ever thought I'd be.

But I would not be joining the list of Cowboy heroes any time soon. I wouldn't join the likes of Roger Staubach and Bob Lilly, two All-American football players I greatly admired. I wouldn't join them because I was an Air Force man. I had a commitment to serve. That's why I went to the Academy and that's why I stayed there all four years.

Someone once asked Scott Thomas, a talented free safety on our 1985 Air Force football team, if he was sad about not having the opportunity to play pro football. He responded, "The best job in the world is being a fighter pilot for the United States of America."

I faced similar questions. When I went to some of the All-American banquets and the post-season all-star games, I had a chance to talk with players from other schools. They'd say things like, "I'm going to the pros. I'm projected to be a first- or second-round pick. I'm going to make all this money and play professional football." Then they'd ask me what I was going to be doing. I'd answer, "I'm going to pilot training in Wichita Falls, Texas, and I'm going to fly jets for the United States Air Force." I thought they'd respond, "Bummer for you, man." But they didn't. They were really impressed with what I was doing.

That was very encouraging for me. It made my situation a little easier to deal with.

It made me realize that Scott Thomas was right. If I couldn't be a Dallas Cowboy, I couldn't do any better than to become a fighter pilot for the United States of America. And that's just what I was about to do.

WORKOUT DRILL

1. What's the toughest thing I've ever done? What value(s) did I learn out of that difficult task?

2. If I had to be as regimented as Chad was in the Air Force, I would (pick one): go crazy, do just fine, get really angry, or become a drill sergeant so I could do this to someone else?

3. What is the most difficult thing for me to do spiritually? (Witnessing, praying as I should, reading the Bible, attending church, talking to other Christians about my faith, doing the right thing, standing up to peer pressure, or something else.)

4. Chad was willing to give up pro football to keep his commitment to the military. What have I had to give up so I could keep a commitment to someone or something else? How did I feel about that choice? Was it the right thing to do?

5. How has God protected me by keeping me from doing something I thought I was ready for but realized later I wasn't?

LOVE AT FIRST SIGHT: CHAD CAUGHT A GLIMPSE OF TAMMY AT A PARTY.

TAMMY

DEDICATED TO THE ONE I LOVE

But Ruth replied, "Don't urge me to leave you or to turn back from you. Where you go I will go, and where you stay I will stay. Your people will be my people and your God my God. Where you die, I will die, and there I will be buried. May the LORD deal with me, be it ever so severely, if anything but death separates you and me."

RUTH 1:16-17

Throughout my lifetime, God has blessed me by guiding me to make good decisions. Attending the Air Force Academy, which led to my becoming a pilot, was one of them. Another was signing a contract with the Cowboys before graduating from the Academy. And, of course, turning my life over to Jesus Christ (which I'll talk about in detail in chapter 6) was an excellent decision because I now have the promise of spending eternity in heaven.

But I can't go any further in this book without telling you about the best decision I ever made pertaining to my life on earth. Of course, like my other decisions, I didn't make this decision alone. God clearly directed me in this one.

I'm talking about my decision to marry Tammy.

Everything I've told you so far has been about my life before I met Tammy. Those events have taught me lessons about commitment, lessons I needed to learn if I was to pursue my life-goals with excellence. They also prepared me to be a good husband for Tammy.

Because I live the life of a professional athlete, I know how important commitment is to my wife. Football takes up a lot of time and I must be able to manage my time appropriately so that I have time to devote to my wife and son. Aside from football, I have many opportunities to make appearances or to make more money. Often, I have to turn these things down so that I have quality time to spend with my family.

Because I am committed to Tammy, I don't do some of the things a lot of men do. I've observed many of my colleagues in professional football doing things that break down their relationships, things they wouldn't do if they chose to live out the commitments they made when they got married. Life in the NFL offers athletes all sorts of opportunities for unsavory behavior, and without a vital sense of commitment to their families, it is easy for many of them to fall right into the pit.

That kind of behavior saddens me. I don't ever want to see a day in which Tammy doubts that I love her with all my heart or suspects that my dedication to her is faltering. In my opinion, a married man isn't a *real* man unless he chooses every day to live out a strong and loving commitment to his wife. It takes more strength of character to do that than it does to give in and cheat.

I hope that as I tell you the story of how Tammy and I met and married, you'll feel challenged to be committed in your marriage relationship, whether you're married now or you hope for marriage in the future.

Love at First Sight (Really!)

As my days wound down at the Air Force Academy, I anticipated the next step in my life journey: Air Force flight training. Although I had a contract with the Cowboys in my files, the next helmet I was scheduled to wear was a jet pilot's headgear, not the silver-and-blue helmet of the 'Boys. I knew where I was going and nothing could distract me from my course.

Or so I thought. Little did I know that I was about to encounter someone who would change my life forever.

Before graduation rolled around, I took a little time to enjoy my last few weeks in Colorado Springs. I wanted to spend time with friends, to connect with them before we all left for flight school.

On one night I'll never forget, I attended a party at a friend's house. A strange thing happened at that party, one of those things you think hap-

pens only in the movies. When I saw Tammy for the first time, I did a double take. You know, where you glance at someone, look away, and then,
wondering if you really saw what you thought you saw, you take a longer,
more intense, second look. But my double take wasn't the strange thing.
Here's what was really unusual: She did the same thing. We did a *double*
double take! *Look. Look away. Look back.* It may sound odd, but it was love
at first sight.

We've all met someone for the first time and felt some attraction.
That had happened to me before, but never anything like this! This double take was different from any other; I knew it was something special,
because I felt an attraction that was more than physical. I could see she
was a beautiful girl, but there was more to it than that. I'm not saying it
was mind blowing or that I knew right away I was going to marry her.
But there was a spark in that first meeting that was unlike anything I'd
ever experienced.

We both tried to play it cool that night, but really, we were falling all
over ourselves—feeling the attraction, wanting to impress the other, but not
knowing how to connect. In fact, we didn't even talk to each other that
night except for a quick "Hi." I had nothing to go on—just a look, a shared
double-take, and a quick greeting—but I felt as if my life would never be
the same.

I know it sounds strange, but that brief meeting at the party was the
beautiful, spark-filled beginning of our relationship. I'm convinced now that
our instant, nonverbal connection had to be God-inspired. We wouldn't have
gotten together any other way, not with me scheduled to leave the area so
soon after our meeting. God was not about to let either of us miss what has
turned out to be a great relationship.

A Slow Start

I went home alone that night, but I had thoughts of Tammy keeping me
company. I wanted to know more about her, who she was, and how I could
see her again.

I wasn't thinking about marriage, only about seeing her again. You see, I didn't think I would be married until I was at least thirty years old, simply because there was so much I wanted to accomplish before I settled down.

But Tammy knew that night. She knew that I was the one she would spend the rest of her life with. Later, she told her friends that I was the man she would marry, that the first time we saw each other at the party she knew that we would be together.

After our first meeting that night, Tammy and I began to take small steps toward each other. We got some help from a mutual friend, a hair stylist who regularly cut my hair and who just happened to be Tammy's best friend. They were both hair stylists in Colorado Springs. Our friend helped us get things rolling. She played mediator for the whole relationship, helping us to keep in contact until I got up enough nerve to ask Tammy for a date.

Our relationship got off to a slow start because I could get away from the Academy only on the weekends. At first, we met in group settings. She'd go out with her friends and I'd go out with my friends, and we'd end up meeting in big groups. I'd always end up talking with our mutual friend and Tammy and I didn't communicate that much. But the cautious looks at each other kept the embers smoldering. It sounds funny, but neither of us wanted to be caught looking at the other.

It took a couple of weeks before I asked her out. I was getting ready to graduate and was attending classes and I couldn't get out on the weekends, so my window of opportunity was pretty small. Finally, I asked her out and she accepted.

Our relationship since that time has been great, but you wouldn't have guessed it by our first date. I took her to see *Caddyshack II*, which was so bad that we walked out of the theater about halfway through the movie. I thought, *Great! What a first impression!* But things got better after that. We went to a restaurant and talked, which is what I wanted to do anyway. It ended up being a great time.

After that, we took advantage of what little time we had before I graduated and left for pilot's training. I was beginning to fall for her hook, line, and sinker. A little flame was lit that would blaze into a bonfire over the long term.

A Forced Separation

Not too long into our relationship, we endured something that would mark our first few years of getting to know each other: separation. Not by choice, you understand. By necessity.

After I graduated, I was assigned to Sheppard Air Force Base in Wichita Falls, Texas, for flight training. I had done some flying at the Academy, but this would be the real thing. I would train in the Euro-NATO program, a joint jet pilot program, in which our NATO allies bring in their pilots to train with American pilots. It was a prestigious assignment. My fascination with flying was sparked at the Academy and now I was finally getting my chance.

But pursuing my dream didn't make leaving my "love at first sight" any easier. I had spent my whole Academy career not seriously dating anyone, and I hadn't anticipated meeting anyone interesting before my departure. But no sooner than I had finally met someone I cared about, I had to leave. It didn't seem fair. But commitment had seen me through difficult situations before, and if I'd ever been committed to anything, I was committed to seeing if this relationship would fulfill all the potential it seemed to have.

So began our long-distance relationship, something that would prepare us for those times in marriage when we would be forced apart due to my Air Force assignments. As I trained in Wichita Falls, Tammy would fly over to visit me or I'd travel to Colorado Springs to see her. We managed such visits once or twice a month. Our whole dating relationship was characterized by this long-distance maneuvering. (We had the phone bills to prove it!)

As we wrote to each other, talked on the phone, and enjoyed our short visits, we realized the truth of what seemed a crazy thought that night of our brief meeting—we were made for each other. Obviously, a long-distance relationship makes it difficult to find out what you want to know about a person. While people who get to see each other regularly can take the time to find out about one another, Tammy and I had to condense the process. At this point, I knew that I cared for Tammy, but I didn't know if she was "the one." It was about six to nine months into our relationship that I finally sat her down and asked her point-blank about things such as children, God, and other things I wanted to know about her. I was happy to find out that we shared so many outlooks on life, including a knowledge of Jesus Christ as our Lord and Savior.

Tammy and I had a wonderful time in each other's company. We laughed together. We dreamed together. We began to know each other's thoughts without speaking a word.

And we fell in love.

One Magic Moment

At this point in the relationship, although I knew I was in love with Tammy, I fought the idea of getting married. I didn't see myself as a husband, and Tammy didn't see herself as a wife, for that matter—at least not at that time. But it didn't take long before I knew that I wanted to marry her, and soon.

Knowing that I'd found my soul mate, the woman I could love and commit to for a lifetime, it didn't take me long to figure out what I had to do. It was time to bring to fruition the truth Tammy heard within herself the night we first met. It was time to pop the question.

One weekend I flew to Colorado Springs to visit my little brother Kent, who was attending the preparatory school at the Air Force Academy. Of course, I also went to see Tammy. Even though my flight didn't touch down until 1:00 A.M., She picked me up at the airport and we drove to her house not saying too much.

After we arrived at Tammy's house, we walked out to her backyard. I'm not much of a romantic guy, but the setting was perfect. It was a starry, moonlit night, and Pike's Peak and the rest of the Rocky Mountain front range towered majestically above us. In the midst of all that beauty, I got down on one knee and proposed to Tammy. It was definitely a magical moment.

I don't know if it was the mountains or me that got to her heart that night, but I do know that Tammy said, "Yes." (Actually, I was pretty sure of what she'd say, but I still had to go through the formality.)

We were engaged. And now it was time for us to prepare to live together in a military setting.

Preparing for Reality

Magical nights don't last forever, and the next day we had to prepare for the realities of marriage in the military. In contrast to the romance of that moonlit night when I proposed, I had to let Tammy know that our first few years of marriage would be rough. I wanted her to understand clearly that when I signed on for flight training, I had committed the next eight years of my life to the Air Force. As my wife, she'd have to be equally dedicated to the commitments I had already made. I described to her as best as I could the military lifestyle, especially how it would impact her as an officer's wife. But having just begun my training, I didn't have a complete idea of what it would be like.

I was trying to prepare her as much as possible for Air Force life. I wanted her to understand that as a pilot I would often be deployed and that there was the risk that if war broke out, chances were high I would not survive.

But Tammy never wavered. She was very positive. She voiced no doubt that she could handle life in the military. "Honey, you've never experienced anything like this," I said. But she replied, "I can get through it."

Of course, I was moving into a new experience myself. While I'd had four years at the Academy to be indoctrinated into the ways and lifestyles of the military, I still had a lot to learn. For one, I'd never been an officer. And for two, I certainly had never been married.

Neither of us knew what to expect, but we knew that we'd be going into the unknown *together*. All we could do was promise to love each other and depend on God's grace to carry us through whatever He had in store for us. I trusted Tammy's strength of character; I felt confident that she wouldn't crack under the pressure of military life.

Our weekend came to an end all too quickly, and even though we still had much to discuss and plan, it was time to part. I had to return to my Air Force commitments while Tammy remained in Colorado Springs. But this time, as I continued to train to make the world safe for democracy, Tammy began planning the day we'd commit to living our lives as one.

Two Weddings for the Price of One

Maybe one of the reasons Tammy and I overcame the adversity of those military years was the fact that we got married twice.

Well, technically, we didn't really marry twice, but we did have two wedding ceremonies.

Soon after Tammy and I got engaged, I was scheduled to ship out in June to serve at a base in England. I wanted Tammy to go with me. To expedite military paperwork so she could ship her stuff to England at the expense of the Air Force, we had to be married. So, on January 26, 1990—much earlier than we had originally planned—we were married at a church in Colorado Springs.

Nobody knew about this wedding except our immediate families. My parents came out, as did Tammy's parents. My sister Kelly and my brother Kent lived in Colorado at the time, so they came too. Kent served as my best man.

A few months later, on June 9, we got "married" again at the Air Force Academy chapel. This time, we pulled out all the stops, inviting all our family and friends to celebrate our commitment to each other. My brother Todd came out for this wedding, and this time he was my best man. Two brothers. Two best men. One beautiful wife. Not many men get to enjoy that kind of wonderful experience!

Wonderful or not, the days surrounding our June ceremony were really stressful for us. Not only were we putting the finishing touches on the ceremony, but we were also preparing to leave for England ten days after our wedding. Beyond that, I was still working hard to learn how to fly the A-10 fighter jet!

Despite the struggles, we survived those preparations and enjoyed an awesome marriage ceremony. Just as the chapel had supplied many calming moments in my freshman year, so did this service provide another opportunity for the majesty of the chapel to quiet my anxious heart. Amid all the turmoil swirling around us in those days, we stood in that chapel together as God reminded us that He was in control of our marriage and would guide us through the times ahead. I had come full circle to the place that had comforted me when I had first committed myself to military life. Our wedding there made everything complete, with Tammy and me recommitting ourselves to each other and reminding ourselves, in this place that had meant so much to me, that we were one.

That breathtaking chapel holds grand memories for me. Several years later, we saw the beauty of that chapel in a new light when our son Chase was baptized there by Jerry Lewis, an Air Force chaplain I'll tell you about later.

Two Keys to a Happy Marriage

As any military person will tell you, military life is not always conducive to keeping married couples together. Time after time, Tammy would find herself all alone while I was off on training missions at undisclosed locations, unable to communicate with her. She eventually learned to handle our separations by either gutting it out alone in England or traveling back to the States to visit family and friends. And even though I had enough to keep me occupied while on my missions, I always longed to be with Tammy. I wanted to invest time and energy into building our marriage.

It's hard to understand how difficult it is to be separated from your spouse until you have to go through it. It's vastly different from being separated from parents and brothers and sisters, because that's expected. But married couples are supposed to be together under the same roof. Part of the deal of marriage is that you stay together.

I missed Tammy terribly when I was separated from her in my military days. Aside from the opportunity to play professional football, that was one of the major reasons I got out of the Air Force when I had the chance. I didn't want to be separated from Tammy or from our children when they came. I couldn't stand the thought of being away from my kids for half of their growing-up years.

It's not easy for any couple to build a strong marriage when the husband and wife spend so much time apart from each other. Yet Tammy and I learned some vital principles that have helped us remain unified even when we were apart, concepts that help us to this day. When the going got tough, our hearts were knit together by our common love for the Lord Jesus Christ, and we worked to incorporate into our lives some biblical principles that can make a marriage work despite the problems.

Two key principles we still emphasize are the two "C's": *Communication* and *Consideration*. We always try to keep our lines of communication open. The book of Proverbs says a lot about them both:

The mouth of the righteous is a fountain of life (10:11).

Hatred stirs up dissension, but love covers over all wrongs (10:12).

A gentle answer turns away wrath (15:1).

A man finds joy in giving an apt reply—and how good is a timely word! (15:23).

One of the biggest aspects of our commitment to one another is the priority of communication. We are committed to listening to one another at all times.

Part of our commitment to good communication is trying to resolve our arguments before we go to sleep at night. We don't sleep on our conflicts; we solve them first. Ephesians 4:26 says, "Do not let the sun go down while you are still angry." Resolving our difficulties immediately keeps them from growing into walls that might separate us.

The second "C" is consideration. This might mean that even if Tammy and I get a little angry with each other, we respect each other enough not to raise our voices. The first part of Ephesians 4:26 says, "In your anger do not sin." We cannot avoid having differences of opinion, but when they occur, we must always stay constructive in what we say, never destructive. Like everybody else, we argue. But we are committed to consideration for each other's feelings. We try to establish good habits. For example I say, "Honey, before we start arguing, let's sit down and pray so that we don't say anything spiteful or vindictive to each other." We get in the right frame of mind before we try to settle conflicts. In that way it becomes profitable.

I must be committed to considering Tammy's feelings in these situations and think about what she's going through. I must always be considerate of her. Of course, she is considerate enough to remind me of this principle quite often!

During our first several years of marriage, we struggled to practice these habits. Of course, in that respect we were no different from any other young married couple. But we faced the added difficulty of not having the time together to work things out. As two people spend more time together, they can work more often on their communication skills and thereby grow together as one. Then marriage can begin to get easier—at least it has for us. But in those first years of marriage, Tammy and I didn't have that time because we were apart so often.

We also faced the difficulty of getting used to living with each other after we were married. Because of our long-distance dating relationship, we hadn't spent much extended time together before we tied the knot. So we were just getting to know each other when we got married. Tammy has said that she never really got to know me until after we were married because our relationship had been long-distance. She realized that a lot was happening to each of us without the other knowing what was going on.

Once we both recognized that fact, we didn't put so many expectations on ourselves and on each other. We were able to step back a bit and let the relationship develop naturally.

Underlying all the principles that we learned in our first years of marriage was this: Maintain a strong dependence on the heavenly Father. Tammy states it clearly when she says, "What kept me going was my faith in God. We knew each other somewhat, but we didn't know each other all that well. But I knew I made a commitment for life, and I loved him. But God's the only thing that kept me going through the tough parts of the military life."

Commitment to God's Plan for Marriage

What has made my marriage to Tammy work is that we are committed to one another and to looking to the Word of God as a model for marriage. We understand that the Bible tells us how marriage is supposed to work.

I'm no marriage expert, but I know that some of the things the world is trying these days simply won't work. For example, I heard from a friend of mine that the newest trend is "starter marriages." These marriages are analogous to starter houses; you get into one of them for a few years until something better comes along. Then you get out.

It's terribly sad to see this kind of thing, because God didn't create marriage that way. When you stand with your spouse-to-be at your wedding ceremony, you make commitments before God to the person you're marrying, to your family, and to your friends. You make a permanent, lifetime commitment. You promise that you'll to do everything you can to make this relationship work. And you promise that you'll never give up, no matter how tough things might get.

If people realized that their wedding vows are commitments before the Almighty God of the universe, they might think twice about having a nonchalant attitude toward marriage. It was God who set down the biblical foundation for marriage. In fact, marriage was one of the first things He created, according to Scripture. He gave us the formula in Genesis 2. A man and a woman leave their parents and become attached to each other. I don't think God would have created marriage in the beginning if He didn't mean for it to be the foundation of our society.

The decline of marriage and family has been the downfall of our society. We have wandered away from the idea of marriage as a lifetime commitment. Instead, people want to do whatever makes them feel good. But that never works; it can't.

It's been proven over and over again since biblical times that the foundation of a society is the family. That means one man and one woman, with the husband serving as the head of the household and the wife (while not subservient to the man) following his lead.

This is biblical truth, God's truth. And I want to be a part of the resurgence of the American family by setting an example of doing what is right with my wife and children. That's the legacy I want to pass on to my kids.

Even outside a military setting, marriage is work, a commitment. But it can be exciting, enjoyable, thrilling work in the context of a firm commitment to your spouse and to God. Marriage isn't always easy, but it does work. And having a woman like Tammy in my life has made all the tough times worth the effort.

WORKOUT DRILL

1. What do I think is the hardest thing a person has to face once he or she is married?

2. Is it possible for people to find "love at first sight"? Is there a danger with that? If so, what?

3. A starry night, the Rocky Mountains, and a big football player on his knees creates quite a romantic picture. What is so valuable about being romantic? Can a relationship work without all that mushy stuff?

4. If I had to come up with two key things that would keep a married couple happy, what would they be? Would I be a help or a hindrance with these things?

5. What are five characteristics I would look for in a mate? (Or . . . what are five wonderful characteristics I appreciate in my spouse?)

BEFORE HE JOINED THE DALLAS COWBOYS, CHAD WAS A U.S. AIR FORCE PILOT.

TROUBLE IN THE MIDDLE EAST

WARTHOG TO THE RESCUE

True grit is making a decision and standing by it, doing what must be done.
No moral man can have peace of mind if he leaves undone what he knows
he should have done.

JOHN WAYNE

In early 1991, while the New York Giants prepared to battle the Buffalo Bills in the Super Bowl, I was preparing for a different battle. Guys like Cornelius Bennett of the Bills, who graduated from Alabama the year before I graduated from the Air Force, were headed for Tampa Bay, Florida, to play the biggest game of their lives. I, on the other hand, was preparing for the possibility of traveling to Iraq to fly in the biggest mission of my life.

Football Is Not War

Many people use war terminology to describe football. We've all heard sportscasters say things like, "It's going to be a war out there this Sunday," or players say, "We're in a battle." We hear football coaches talk about battle plans and strategies as they prepare their teams for the big game.

But in fact the two are nothing alike. When I play football, I push people around, run into them, and sometimes manhandle quarterbacks. I never intend to hurt anyone. But during war, injuring and sometimes killing people is part of the deal.

No matter what level of football you're playing, it's still a game. But flying a jet in combat is not a game. It's a life-and-death situation. If someone make a mistake in a football game, no one dies. But if a pilot errs in flying a fighter jet, he can crash and burn. You're risking your life every time you take off in a jet. You can lose your life if your jet malfunctions, if another pilot doesn't see you, or even if you run into a flock of birds.

If there is a meaningful similarity between football and flying a jet, it's this: Flying your jet has to become second nature. Your plane has to be a part of you. You have to be ready for anything, because if you're not, it could cost you everything.

In the Air Force, I flew the A-10 Thunderbolt II fighter jet, affectionately known as the Warthog for its less than lovely appearance (it's no sleek F-16 by any stretch of the imagination). The A-10's other nickname is Tankbuster because it is used primarily to take out the enemies' tanks. When you fly a tankbuster in combat, your job is to take out as much of the enemies' ground assets as possible, and that means the possibility of taking out some-one's son. It's not a pleasant thought, but then neither is the thought of let-ting an aggressor like Iraq overtake a country like Kuwait, or ravage a people like the Kurds.

An A-10 Warthog is a bit like a flying machine gun. The whole plane is built around a thirty-millimeter Gatling gun mounted in the nose of the fighter. That gun shoots depleted uranium-tipped bullets. The whole weapons system is about the size of a Volkswagen Beetle, and the plane looks like a big grasshopper. The A-10's wings carry anything from bombs to Maverick missiles.

With the thirty-millimeter gun in the nose of the plane alone, a pilot can shoot and kill a tank from more than two miles away. With the Maverick missiles, a pilot can hit a target from three-and-a-half to seven miles away. Maverick missiles are "fire and forget" weapons, guided by either an electro/optical or laser-guided sensor in the nose of the missile. A mini-television screen in the cockpit shows a pilot his target. The pilot aims the missile toward the target, locks it in, shoots, and gets out of there. All of this happens in five to seven seconds. You don't want to expose yourself too long to enemy threats.

Fortunately for me as an A-10 Warthog pilot, the best thing about this jet is its survivability. The pilot sits in a titanium "bathtub" for protection. That jet could take a twenty-millimeter shell point-blank, and the shell wouldn't penetrate the cockpit.

War Is Declared

As tensions heated up in the Middle East with the United States involved in Operation: Desert Shield, war seemed imminent. I was stationed in Bentwaters, England, training in an A-10 Warthog. Tammy was with me.

On January 16, 1991, the United States declared war on Iraq. I'll never forget where I was when I heard the news. I was in Germany stationed at the Leipheim Air Base, doing our standard forward deployment along the East-West German border. I woke up early that morning with the gut-level feeling that I should turn on CNN. I watched President George Bush give his speech to America explaining our actions and our intentions. I was very excited and wanted to get over there to the Gulf, just like every other fighter pilot.

Even after the war began, though, our squadron remained in England. Other units of Tankbusters were deployed to take care of the Iraqis, but we were not yet called on to do battle. Ever since I had graduated from the Academy, I had wanted to test my skills in combat. I was more than ready to go, if the call came.

Everybody in our squadron wanted to go, to test ourselves against the Iraqis. We thought we should go to the Persian Gulf before other squadrons, but we had Cold War commitments in Europe—to protect the former East/West German border. But since that border was no longer in existence, we were antsy to see some Persian Gulf action.

Trouble over the Mediterranean

Finally, on April 6, with the hostilities of Operation: Desert Storm almost over, we got the call to head for action. It was 5:00 A.M., and I got a call from my squadron commander to come in and start planning a secret mission.

After a long planning session, I raced home to prepare. I packed some bags, consoled my wife, called my folks in Iowa, and took off for our squadron briefing. I couldn't tell my parents or Tammy where I was headed, and I found that difficult. But I was thrilled with the opportunity and felt comforted in knowing that Tammy was in the control tower watching me take off shortly after midnight the next morning. I knew my family back home and my wife were praying for me as I turned my plane toward Turkey.

I was excited. This is what I had trained for. I was like a kid coming downstairs Christmas morning to see all the presents. But it was hard on Tammy that I couldn't tell her where we were going (although she probably had a pretty good idea, given what was going on at the time) and because we didn't know how long we'd be gone. Fortunately, other wives there had husbands who were doing the same thing. Still, she didn't have her family there for support.

It takes about eight hours to fly from England to Turkey. To get there we flew south to the Mediterranean around the boot of Italy, over Sicily, and then over the Mediterranean to Incirlik, Turkey. But about five-and-a-half hours into the flight, I started having problems with my aircraft. The flight instruments indicated oil pressure fluctuations in my number two engine. Apparently, a faulty seal in the engine was causing me to lose oil. Finally, I had to shut down that engine, which meant I was flying on one engine over the Mediterranean Sea.

Any time you're flying single-engine in that sort of aircraft, which is underpowered to begin with, there's a threat to your safety. Plus, we were flying over the ocean, and it was spring when the weather is unpredictable. But I remained calm. I said to myself, "I've done this a hundred times in simulation."

We were flying in a four-ship formation, so my wingman and I diverted to the north and headed for a naval facility on the island of Crete while the other two pilots continued on. As we neared the island, we tried to talk to the controller, but he was Greek and didn't speak English well. Not only did we have translation problems, but the Greeks were celebrating their Easter holiday, so they had minimal staff on duty at the base.

I tried to explain to the controller that I was in an emergency situation, that I was flying on one engine, and that I had hot munitions on board. "I need to land now," I told the controller. But he responded, "I don't understand, tell me more."

I didn't have time to talk. Thank God the weather was clear, because all my wingman and I could do was visually clear the area to make sure there was no other traffic. I set myself on a single-engine pattern and headed for the runway.

The difficult thing about landing the A-10 is that its engines are outside the fuselage, so you get a lot of yaw, meaning the nose of the plane veers left or right with the addition or deletion of power. You have to compensate for power deletions with the use of your rudders and be careful with using the remaining engine throttle to add power. It's tricky, and with one engine, you don't have a lot of power to respond. As I said, the plane is under-powered to begin with, so you don't want to come in too slowly; if you're not carrying enough speed, you may smack the ground. The key thing is to control the nose of the plane and keep it on line.

By the time I attempted this landing, I was extremely tired. I hadn't slept since I had received that call at 5:00 the previous morning. But with all that was going on, I was pretty wired. All I had to do was to concentrate on getting that plane down. My training was invaluable; I had done so many simulated single-engine landings that I knew just what to do.

Whether the controller was ready or not, I had committed to landing the plane. With my wingman giving me guidance and encouragement, I set my Warthog down on that island runway and coasted to a safe stop.

I hadn't made it to Turkey yet, but I was already involved in some unexpected excitement!

The next day another pilot flew in and I flew his plane to Turkey while a mechanic arrived to fix mine. The mechanic discovered what I had expected him to find: a leaky seal that had been spewing oil before I shut the engine down.

Operation: Provide Comfort

Once I arrived in Turkey, I learned of our twofold mission. First, we took off from Incirlik Air Base in Aduna, Turkey, to fly escort for the airlift aircraft that were dropping relief supplies to the Kurds. Then we flew reconnaissance missions over Iraq. We monitored the Iraqis, making sure they obeyed all the restrictions of the no-fly exclusion zone rules. This deployment was called Operation: Provide Comfort. Instead of using our mean, lean, flying machines as weapons of destruction, we used them to bring help and hope to the Kurdish people.

It took plenty of preparation to make our missions successful. Before we even thought about taking off, we spent a lot of time preparing terrain maps. Those maps helped us navigate our course to northern Iraq and plot our reconnaissance around the country. We had to chart a course from Turkey, across the northern part of Syria, and then dip down into northern Iraq. After preparing our maps, we'd study our intelligence reports to learn of all the threats to our missions, such as antiaircraft, surface-to-air missiles, troops in the area, and if there were any hostile activities in the area at the time.

We also had to calculate our fuel levels and arrange our air-to-air refueling tracts, get our internal navigation systems set up, make sure we were familiar with our geographical points, get our call signs, check our takeoff times, and record all our takeoff and landing data.

Initially, we escorted C-130s, which are huge tactical airlift planes that were dropping supplies to the Kurds. But before we could provide help to the Kurds, we had to find out where they were. We often had to fly reconnaissance missions just to find them. Once we found them, we'd get in touch with the C-130 crews to find out where we would meet with them to escort them to a drop point. And we'd discuss what tactics to use in escort.

When we first began these missions, it took quite awhile to prepare for them. When I first arrived in Turkey, I had to do this all in a day's time because the next day was my first mission. But once you've completed one mission, it's easier the second, third, fourth, and fifth times around.

Once I created a routine for my missions, flying got a little boring. But there were some highlights, such as flying over the Tigris and Euphrates Rivers in northern Turkey and Iraq. I looked for Noah's Ark when we refueled air-to-air over Mount Ararat. Also, we took off about twenty-five miles from Tarsus, the apostle Paul's birthplace.

Midair refueling was an adventure, too. Our long flights made this a necessity, but many pilots don't like it because they don't do it that often and therefore don't feel comfortable with the procedure. And sometimes, depending upon the weather, the tanker was tough to find. A couple of times the only information we had about a tanker's location was that it was within a five-mile diameter "clear area" in the middle of the scattered cloud banks. We had to find this tanker based on a radio beacon that gave us a general idea as to the general direction we had to fly and the distance between us and the tanker. We had to pick up the tanker visually.

Finding the tanker isn't the only difficult part of this procedure. Once I found the tanker, I had to join up with it to refuel. To do this, I'd try to work out the geometry, because the tanker might be coming directly at me. In those cases I'd have to squeeze in behind the tanker while it and my aircraft were both traveling 250-300 knots. There is no precise, surefire method. Basically, you use the TLAR Principle: "That looks about right."

Once we got to our general destination in Iraq, we didn't always know exactly where we were supposed to be. Our Internal Navigation System (INS) could drift up to two-and-a-half miles per hour, so three to four hours into the mission, we could be off by five to seven-and-a-half miles. Because of this, by the time we dropped down from our cruising altitude, we had to use our maps to determine our location.

At this point in our mission, we'd fly by using visual keys, looking at the map, and using the clock and landmarks on the ground to decide where we were. In our training as A-10 pilots, we'd fly 250-500 feet above the ground, holding a map and looking for railroad crossings, tree lines, and anything else that might tell us where we were. Because we had to operate this way, flying in Iraq and Turkey was extremely exciting.

As we gained our bearings in this fashion, we also had to keep our eyes open for threats and to pick up the C-130s. We met up with the C-130s at a particular point, then we'd escort them to protect them from threats, recomb the area, and pick up where the Kurds were. Then the C-130s would drop down and release their relief supplies, and we'd escort them up again. After completing these tasks, we'd come back out, refuel, and head for

Turkey. Each mission took six hours. It was a pretty lonesome six hours, because the A-10 is a single-seater. We had to do everything solo. But as I said, we had been well-trained. I had spent four years learning to fly jets well enough to lead another wingman into any situation we might encounter.

I enjoyed participating in these missions to help the Kurds, but I found the experience frustrating, too. We'd been commissioned to protect the Kurds in northern Iraq, but the Turks were bombing them in the Turkish territory. We could see the Turks rolling in and dropping bombs on the Kurds while we were more than twenty-five to thirty miles south protecting the Kurds in northern Iraq.

Our missions didn't meet with much resistance other than occasional small fire by the overzealous Kurds or Iraqis or whoever was in the area. Our rules of engagement were such that we weren't supposed to dip below 5,000 feet when there were threats. Since we flew so high, the energy of the bullets dissipated by the time they reached us. So we were safe above that altitude.

Of course, we flew over antiaircraft batteries all the time, but the Iraqis believed that if they fired on us they'd experience a world of hurt. Fortunately, they didn't know our rules for firing on them. To fire, we first had to leave the area, talk to the AWACs (radar planes flying high overhead), who would then talk to the commanding general back at Incirlik just to get permission to alleviate the threat.

Although the Warthogs were commissioned as escort planes on humanitarian relief missions, the Tankbuster played a big part in our success during the early days of combat. In fact, you could say the A-10 was the hero of the Gulf War. It did the most damage.

With the A-10, fighting the Iraqis became like shooting fish in a barrel. The A-10 would loiter ten thousand to fifteen thousand feet and roll in, acquire a target, release its ordinance, and do that over and over. The Tankbuster was one of two planes that the Iraqi soldiers said they feared the most. They feared the A-10 for its assault on tanks and the B-52 for its carpet bombing capabilities.

I myself never fired on anybody during my time in the Air Force. If necessary, I would have, but only if there had been the need. Nobody wants to kill anybody just for the sake of doing so. The Air Force doesn't need bloodthirsty pilots.

Over the span of one year, I spent two three-month deployments flying humanitarian missions over Iraq. Serving in Operation: Provide Comfort is one of the most valuable experiences I've ever had. My commitment to the Air Force and to training paid off in the opportunity to serve weaker and less-fortunate people in another country. If I had to do it all over again, I would.

How to Get to Dallas from England

All the while I had been in the Air Force, I continued to prepare my body for the possibility that I might someday get to play for the Cowboys. I didn't play any football, but I played other sports and lifted weights to add more bulk and strength to my body.

The working out also benefited me as a pilot. Physical strength and endurance are important for pilots because they must be able to stand the G-forces and the physical strain of flying. The Air Force encouraged my training habits, so I was preparing myself not only for the possibility of playing pro football, but for the reality of being a pilot.

Even when we were done with Operation: Provide Comfort and 1991 faded into 1992, I knew it would be a long time before I could switch uniforms from the Air Force fighter-pilot jumpsuit to the Dallas Cowboys football uniform.

Tammy and I had been in England for two years, and I knew I had at least one more year of service in England (even though the brass was closing RAF Bentwaters and RAF Woodbridge, the twin bases that we called home). I had to begin to actively look for a follow-up assignment.

Around this time, the United States had begun to reduce the size of its military force. With the end of the Cold War and the fall of communism in Eastern Europe, the U.S. was downsizing the military. For me, this meant an immediate waiver of my pilot training commitment, three years off my time in the Air Force. Still, I was only at the four-year point and I knew I had to remain in the service until the summer of 1993.

One option I pursued was to return to the Air Force Academy as a coach. I called Coach Fisher DeBerry and asked him if I could coach football for a year. Working on the staff of the Air Force Academy would fulfill my final year of military commitment because I'd still be employed by the Air Force, and I could use the time to get back into the game. This was in early 1992.

Coach DeBerry said, "Yeah, come on. We'd love to have you!"

The prospect of coaching at the Academy was exciting for me. Coach DeBerry is a Christian man who showed commitment to me when I played for him. He knew me as a player and as a person. He knew my character. I played for him for four years and I would love to help him just as much as he helped me.

So that's what I planned to do. I was going to sacrifice flying because I had fulfilled my commitment, and I was going to move on. I would coach football and try to play football when the opportunity came.

Little did I know that the opportunity would come much sooner than I had thought.

While Tammy and I were still in England (preparing to move back to the States), we received a phone call from a friend at about 2:00 A.M. He didn't realize the time difference, but he wanted me to know that the Air Force had just announced a new policy. Air Force officers weren't getting out fast enough, so they were waiving two years of the Air Force Academy commitment.

In other words, I was eligible to get out immediately!

For a moment, I thought I was dreaming. I tried to get back to sleep, but it was a restless sleep. I was excited. I slept for maybe another hour the rest of the night. Already I was making plans about what I was going to do.

Later that morning, I called some friends in the States and asked, "Is this for real?" They said, "Yes."

So it was true. For the first time since I was drafted by the Cowboys, there was a very real chance I would have an opportunity to move to Dallas to play professional football.

But still I wrestled with what I was going to do. Commitment was important to me, and I didn't know what to think about my remaining responsibility to the Air Force. Everyone who knew me knew how much I wanted to get out and play for the Cowboys, yet they also knew that I would not be happy if I felt I had shirked my responsibility.

While I was talking to a senior captain (the weapons officer in our squadron) about this one day, he said, "Hey, you're not quitting the Air Force. You're going on to a different phase of your life." So I began to look at it from that perspective. I realized that he was right; God had another plan for me.

I also talked with Fisher DeBerry because I had already made a commitment to coach for him and I intended to fulfill that commitment if he still wanted me. I called him from a pay phone from the officers' building where we were staying. I said, "Coach, this is Chad Hennings. I just got a call from MPC (the Air Force's assignment branch) and I'm eligible to get out of the Air Force now. I just wanted to clear it with you first. Do you still want me to coach? What do you think?"

Coach DeBerry just chuckled and said, "Don't even let it enter your head. Chad, you'd do far more good for us by playing professional football than you could by coming here. It's the best for you. Do that, by all means. Don't even think about it. God bless you."

I could have been happy coaching at the Air Force Academy, and it may still be an option down the road. I don't necessarily like the recruiting aspect of coaching, but I enjoy interaction with the players. But because Coach DeBerry supported my dreams of playing in the NFL, he was willing to release me from that commitment.

Immediately I called my agent, Jack Mills, the one who had helped me negotiate my contract with the Cowboys almost four years earlier. I asked him to contact the Cowboys to see if they were still interested in me as a player. They still owned the rights to me (they had paid me $25,000 for those rights) and I was eager to start making their investment pay off.

Jack called me back the next day at 2:00 A.M. (Do you see a pattern developing here?) and said, "If you're still interested, can you be on a flight out of London at 10:00 tomorrow morning to fly back to Dallas for a work-out with the Cowboys?"

Could I? Of course I could! But before I could get on that plane, I had my work cut out for me. I had to work out all my leave orders and I had less than twenty-four hours to get it done. I called my commander and said, "Hey, can you work on this for me?" He replied, "Yeah, don't worry about it. We'll take care of you."

Through this whole episode in my life, the thing that stands out is how everyone bent over backward to help. That's something I'll never forget.

Before I left, Air Force chaplain Jerry Lewis came over to our house and prayed with me for a safe journey and for me to do my best. I had no idea what to expect once I arrived in Dallas, so Lewis prayed for me to have the strength to do my best in whatever was demanded of me.

By 10:00 the next morning, I was on a commercial airliner heading for Texas, while Tammy stayed behind in England.

Jimmy, Jerry, and the Media

I arrived in Dallas on a Friday evening. The Cowboys put me up in a hotel and I met with team owner Jerry Jones and his son Stephen, who was team vice president, and some other people on the Cowboys' administrative staff. I chatted with them and told them some of my war stories.

That night, with all the excitement, the seven-hour time change, and the jet lag, I couldn't sleep. So I prayed. I read the book of Job; it motivated me because of all the strife and turmoil he endured. Even though my stress came from positive sources, I felt I could relate to Job's feelings. God put him to the test, and he passed it. For me, the test was going to be the physical, emotional, and spiritual test of "Am I ready to do this? Am I ready for the change of occupation? Am I ready to go out and perform at a high level, to do certain things I haven't done in four or five years?" I said to myself, "This guy Job had everything taken from him—his possessions, his children, his name, but still he had faith in God. So the least I can do is go out and try my best, and whether or not it works out, Glory to God!"

Living a Dream

The next morning I was on the field, working out for the Dallas Cowboys! Ever since I had first realized in my senior year of college that I might be good enough to play in the pros, I had dreamed of this opportunity. And here I was, hoping to fulfill that dream. But I wasn't attempting this under the most ideal circumstances. I was tired, disoriented, and not in exceptional football shape.

Again, I didn't know what to expect from this tryout. I assumed I would work out in front of the strength and conditioning coach and maybe my position coach. But when I arrived, Jerry Jones and his administrative staff, the entire coaching staff, and several members of the media were all there. I could see that this was going to be nerve-racking.

I had been playing intramural softball and basketball and doing a little running, so I was in decent shape. But this was different. This was the National Football League. And I hadn't run a forty-yard dash since college.

So I warmed up and began my evaluation. I ran the forty-yard dash, and they clocked me at 4.8 seconds—not too bad for a guy my size and especially for a guy running in Air Force-issue jogging shoes! But after I finished running, I turned around to look back, and I rolled my ankle. It swelled up immediately and started to turn black and blue.

My first reaction was, "Why now?" But it never crossed my mind that I would allow this to slow me down. I had no choice but to gut it out. I had sprained the same ankle playing basketball at the Air Force base and I had to sit out for a week. I couldn't fly because I couldn't extend the same foot. I knew this wasn't as bad, that I could get through it. I didn't want the coaches even to know about it. I didn't want them to entertain any negative thoughts about me whatsoever. I wasn't going to let the Dallas coaches say, "This kid sprained his ankle running a forty-yard dash. What's going to happen when he has to play?"

I went over to the trainer and asked him to tape my ankles. I didn't tell him why. I just said, "Please tape my ankles, because I don't want to twist them." It was true. I surely didn't want to twist them now that I had already rolled one! I was wearing tube socks and I told the trainer just to tape over the socks.

After I ran, the coaches wanted me to do some agility drills. I calmly said a prayer before I began that God would give me peace of mind to do my best. I wasn't nervous. Instead, I felt confident, at peace. I completed the agility drills and then the coaches asked me to do a drill designed for college prospects at the combines, where seniors are tested for their physical skills. I ran one of the fastest times they had clocked that year. They also asked me to do a bench press for them, which was fine with me because I had been lifting weights anyway.

When the workout was over, they let me know they were happy with what I had showed them. Smiles lit up everywhere. "Hey, as soon as you get out of the Air Force, come on down," they said. "We want you to come here."

With that encouragement I headed back to England to prepare for our move to Dallas.

I'm glad I went back to England after my tryout because the Dallas media went crazy. They wrote articles that said, in effect, "This guy's going to come up and be the savior of the Dallas defense." Jimmy Johnson made a comment that I had dropped out of heaven.

Within a month, I'd be back in the United States, preparing myself for training camp. And the Cowboys would find out how much I had to learn before I could save their defense!

I'd like to give myself the credit, but I can't. It wasn't me; it was God who had worked through me. All I had done was to remain committed to something, even if it was only a dream. But now I was excited.

I was going to be a Dallas Cowboy!

Military Debriefing

My military days were over, but the experience will live with me for the rest of my life.

It will live with me in one sense because of the honors I received while serving my country. First, everyone who served in the Gulf conflict received the South West Asia Campaign medal. Also, because of what we did for the Kurds, our unit received a humanitarian award and an outstanding unit award. Also, I was given a safety award for that single-engine landing in Crete. I received an Emeritus Service Award, which you get if you have a clean record after completing one tour successfully. And I received a longevity medal for being in the service a certain number of years.

In another sense, my military experience will live with me because of what it taught me. There are so many of life's lessons that I don't think I could have learned anywhere else than in the Air Force. What I learned gives me a mental advantage in so many situations, both on the football field and off.

I've learned to handle adversity through the many difficulties I faced while flying. I've learned a lot about paying attention to detail—about doing the little things right the first time. I learned how to formulate a game plan for accomplishing a certain goal. I also gained a vast amount of knowledge, the skill of memorization, and the ability to adapt to change.

Flexibility is perhaps one of the biggest things I learned in the Air Force. There's an Air Force saying that goes, "What's the key to air power? Flexibility." We'd be flying in difficult situations and suddenly everything would change. We'd have to adapt to a different game plan if we were to accomplish our mission. Yes, the Air Force taught me flexibility. And flexibility would turn out to be an important part of my career in NFL football (I'll discuss that further in chapter 7).

Oh, yes. There's one other sense in which my time in the military will live with me for the rest of my life. During my military years, Tammy and I made a spiritual commitment that has brought us closer to Jesus Christ than we've ever been. It's hard to describe the difference it has made and will continue to make in our lives, but I'd like to try, because I want you to enjoy the happiness that Jesus offers.

WORKOUT DRILL

1. Chad Hennings proudly answered the call to serve his country as a fighter pilot. Have I ever considered what I might owe my country in some kind of service?

2. It takes faith and courage to sit inside a plane, knowing the enemy would like nothing better than to see that craft go down in flames. What challenge am I facing that is going to take faith and courage? How should I prepare for that challenge?

3. What is the value of being tested by a dangerous situation? How can that help me later in my life?

4. Throughout his time in the military, Chad continued to prepare for the day he might get a chance to try out for the Cowboys. What kinds of things am I working toward as long-range goals—things I know I can't accomplish now but want to do later?

5. How flexible am I? When I need to make changes in my life, am I happy about it or bothered by it?

CHAPLAIN LEWIS HELPED THE HENNINGS' REDEDICATE THEIR LIVES.

CHAPTER SIX

◀ A REDEDICATION ▶

THE BEST THING THAT EVER HAPPENED TO US

The healthy and strong individual is the one who asks for help when he needs it—
whether he's got an abscess on his knee or in his soul.

ANONYMOUS

In the den of my home, I have a lot of special mementos from my years of football and flying.

I have game footballs that I've earned while with the Cowboys.

I have my Outland Trophy (which is really just a plaque, by the way, but don't tell anyone).

I have my miniature Vince Lombardi trophies that symbolize the Cowboys' Super Bowl victories.

I have models of the A-10 Warthog to remind me of my years of service to my country.

There's not much anywhere else in the house to suggest that I play football in the NFL or that I flew in the Air Force, but this room is special because of these reminders of my careers. I don't display these items to show off or to prove anything to anybody, but to remind myself of how grateful I should be that God has allowed me to enjoy such incredible experiences. I realize that not many people get to fly jets for the United States Air Force or play football in the National Football League. And God has blessed me with the privilege of doing both.

This den full of memories captures some of the most incredible moments in my life. But no plaque or trophy or autographed photo or game ball can adequately symbolize the greatest thing that has happened to Tammy and me.

Now, I don't want to minimize any of the remarkable and wonderful events in our lives. For instance, the birth of our son Chase has to be, humanly speaking, our favorite day. We cherish him and what he brings to our family, so I would never minimize the importance of God's gift of our son. And, of course, our marriage is another clear evidence of divine blessing.

Yet Tammy and I both know that without a strong, vibrant relationship with Jesus Christ, our lives would lack the substance, depth, and spiritual significance that make each day outstanding. For both of us, our salvation is the starting point for everything that is truly good.

What a Difference Jesus Makes!

Tammy's walk with Jesus Christ began in her church back in Colorado, and mine started as I was growing up in Iowa. Our shared faith was one of the traits that drew us together after we met and exchanged the double takes.

But to tell the truth, our faith was not a high priority for a long time in our marriage. Although we each knew Jesus Christ as Savior, we were not seriously committed to living for Him. We loved Him, but we weren't dedicated to serving Him as Lord every day and in every way.

I had a Christian foundation. I was raised to go to church, attend catechism and confirmation classes, read the Bible, and pray. I can remember riding a lawn mower when I was ten or eleven years old, singing hymns and having conversations with God. I remember all sorts of incidents in my life that demonstrated a knowledge of God.

I knew Jesus Christ, but I didn't pursue a close, personal relationship with Him. I hadn't made that kind of commitment.

At least that's the way it was until one life-changing day in England during our time in the military. That's when things really started to take off for us spiritually. We haven't been the same since.

The man behind the change was our military chaplain, Jerry Lewis. Jerry was no ordinary chaplain. He was a charismatic leader who eagerly got involved in the lives of the men in our fighter squadron. He first got my attention when I observed his competitiveness. Even though he was a chaplain—which basically requires that you be a nice, gentle person—he played intramural basketball with us. And whenever he played, he played to win. I respected that.

But I also respected him because he was never afraid to talk about his faith.

Chaplain Lewis had two Sunday services on the base—a traditional service and a more contemporary one. Occasionally, Tammy and I attended the more contemporary service. At one of these services, shortly after returning from my first deployment in Turkey, something happened to me that changed the course of my life.

Tammy had been reluctant to attend Jerry's Bible studies while I was away. She'd see Jerry often and he'd always invite her to Bible study. But Tammy has always been a person with an "I can do it on my own" mentality. And even though she had the Lord in her life, she didn't let a lot of people get close to her. As she said, "I don't know if I was a glutton for loneliness and punishment, but I spent a lot of time at home alone during the three months Chad was off in Turkey flying in Operation: Provide Comfort. So, every time Jerry would ask me to join the Bible study while Chad was gone, I declined."

When I got back from Turkey, both Tammy and I felt the need for some support, so we decided to attend one of the contemporary services.

Although I didn't understand it at the time, I had observed some things while on deployment that made me ripe for a change. During my time in Turkey and Iraq, I saw for the first time what a Muslim country was like. I discovered that many Christians in that part of the world were still persecuted for their faith.

I had heard stories from Turkish Christians who attended church on base about some of the persecution they had seen and felt. There were stories of Christians being beaten by Muslims or about Christians being murdered for their faith. Base life sheltered us from what was happening outside; the base was like a little America. But when you left the base, you saw the towns and the country, and you saw the poverty of the people. Yet through everything—the persecution and the poverty—the Turkish Christians demonstrated a vibrancy in their faith, a true commitment to Jesus Christ.

To this point, I had always taken my Christian faith for granted. I had always tried to be a good person. I tried to go to church on Sunday, to treat people right, to do the right thing. I always considered myself a Christian because that's the way I was raised. But when I left home and got into college, I got deeply involved in athletics, going out with my friends, and everything else that characterizes the college lifestyle. I got too busy for God, and I would say that during that time I fell away a little bit. I never went into big-time rebellion, but my relationship with God became stagnant.

But after observing this vibrancy of faith in the face of persecution, I suddenly began to see this idea of trusting Christ differently. I was challenged by the thought that some people were risking their lives for the gospel.

As I sat in that service (the one I attended soon after returning from Turkey) with Tammy by my side and the congregation singing "The Old Rugged Cross," all this came to a head for me. I realized that I had been ignorant of what was going on around me spiritually. It suddenly dawned on me that as a Christian, I was in the middle of a battle—a spiritual battle. And I could easily fall along the wayside if I didn't completely commit myself to Jesus Christ.

Out of nowhere, there was a huge burst of emotion inside of me. I had a huge lump in my throat and tears began to well up in my eyes. I was so overcome that I couldn't finish the song. Tammy continued to sing as I sat there overwhelmed with unexpected and unfamiliar emotions. This was the first time in my life that I recognized the Holy Spirit working within me. It was as if I were being smacked in the face by something that no one else could see. It was an indescribably wonderful feeling.

As I sat there, I thought about those Turkish Christians and what they had to endure for their faith. I thought about my own spiritual condition and about the stagnation that had marked my spiritual life since I left home. Then it hit me: I didn't have that commitment to Jesus Christ that I should have had.

I realized that being a Christian is more than just going to church on Sundays. I realized that I couldn't be dedicated to Jesus for just one day, then turn off the switch for the rest of the week. I wasn't leading a bad lifestyle, but

I also wasn't taking my faith seriously throughout the whole week. It struck me that I didn't have to be leading what we think of as a sinful lifestyle (like being an alcoholic or being promiscuous) to miss out on a commitment to God. I realized that I could be a good person at heart but still not have that daily walk.

I knew it was time for surrender, time to give my life completely over to Jesus Christ, and time to make the ultimate commitment I could ever make. If I was in a battle, I needed to fight it wholeheartedly. I prayed right there, "Here I am, Lord. Do with me what You will. Thy will be done. I'm here for Your service. Whatever You want me to do, that's what I'm going to do."

Later, as I was driving home, I talked with Tammy about what had happened during the church service. I explained to her that I had been totally overcome by the Holy Spirit. As it turns out, she'd been going through this process while I was in Turkey. She didn't have the kind of experience I did, but she was going through some dramatic changes of her own. It's amazing how the process of spiritual awakening started the same year with both of us.

From that day on, I began to grow spiritually. I rededicated myself to Christ and began to take my spiritual growth seriously. That's when we started attending Bible studies, taking an active role in reading the Bible, and witnessing to other people. And the process continues.

A Spiritual Mentor

After my experience at the church service, Jerry Lewis became my mentor and spiritual partner, guiding me in the ways I needed to grow. Jerry taught me a lot about what it means to be a Christian. He didn't make it easy on me, either. I discovered that just as I had trained rigorously to learn to fly jets and to play football, I had to train to become a strong Christian. Just as I have to pursue disciplined habits to make my body ready for each season of football, I have to be disciplined in my pursuit of the Lord. I have to make daily habits of prayer, Bible study, listening to God, and pursuing relationships with other Christians.

And Jerry challenged me to do one other thing: Tell other people about my faith. This was difficult for me at first. I wasn't afraid before, but I always felt uncomfortable talking about my faith with anyone. Sure, I could talk about God. At times, I talked theology with people in my squadron, even with those who didn't believe in God. But actually sitting down and talking with someone about my faith, witnessing about Jesus Christ, was something I had a hard time doing.

But I've found out how valuable telling other people about my faith really is to my own spiritual growth. And once I realized that, it wasn't long before I was standing up in front of people, testifying about Jesus Christ.

It has been a gradual process for me. After my recommitment, I was able to get up in front of a crowd of maybe a dozen people and tell them about my faith. But as time has gone on and as I have grown in my boldness to talk about the Lord, He has given me the opportunity to speak to even larger crowds. Since then, I've given my testimony in front of a thousand people at one time. I had given speeches before, but never like this.

That demonstrated to me how God works with us. God was with me in the beginning and He knew what I could handle at the time (which wasn't much). But He allowed me to take the baby steps, to start small and work my way up. It's like training for a marathon. I couldn't go out and run a marathon right away, but if I have that commitment to train every day, there will come a time when I can finish the race.

Recognizing God's Leading

With my recommitment in England as a backdrop, I can look back now and see how Christ has led me all the way through my life. For instance, I can look at how I came to the Cowboys and thank God for how He worked in my life. He worked his agenda. I know now that there are reasons I didn't have the smooth road to the pros that most players enjoy. For one thing, I had to go through my military experience so I could become a stronger Christian. If I hadn't gone to Turkey, I wouldn't have seen the persecution and been challenged to become more committed to my faith. For another, my body needed that extra time to mature so I could face the rigors of professional football.

That's what is so interesting about the way God works. He deals with us as individuals. What was necessary for me may not be necessary for others. God leads His children down different paths according to their unique physical, emotional, mental, and spiritual needs.

God knew all along what I needed to grow in my knowledge of Him. And he guided me every step of the way—even when I didn't realize it.

And I'm still growing. Tammy and I are nowhere near where we should be spiritually or where we'll be when the Lord is done with us, but we're on the right road. And as long as we stay on that road, we'll reach the right destination. How can I be so sure? Because God promises that we can be "confident of this, that he who began a good work in you will carry it on to completion until the day of Christ Jesus" (Philippians 1:6).

That's something to be excited about!

An Eternal Commitment

We've talked a lot about commitment in this book, but there's one thing we all have to understand. A commitment to sports is nothing compared with a commitment to the Lord. For one thing, one deals with eternal life or death, heaven or hell; the other is just a game.

Nevertheless, you go about commitment to sports and a commitment to the Lord in the same way: systematically. Commitment is daily discipline, something that requires training. In both realms, stumbling blocks appear in front of you. In the spiritual arena, there's Satan, who tries to defeat you in any way he can. On the football field, there are teammates trying to take your position or opponents trying to defeat you.

You have to live a life of commitment if you want victory over the enemy in either arena.

Let's say you play on a basketball team. Your coach wants you to be extremely committed during the season. He may require you to work hard in practice, attend team meetings, and be there on time for road trips. He'll also ask you to avoid doing anything that will harm your body or make you ineligible academically (if you're playing school sports). But he may also ask you to be committed during the off-season. He may want you to spend a good part of your summer running, lifting weights, or practicing your shooting. When you're a kid, those commitments sound like they last forever, even though they're over before you know it.

But a commitment like that is nothing compared with the commitment to Jesus Christ we make as believers. As Christians, we commit to Christ for eternity, even though in human terms we can't grasp what eternity is. But keep in mind that the alternative to living with Christ in heaven for eternity is being in hell for the same eternity.

For me, my commitment to Christ far surpasses any other commitment I could make to anybody or anything else. What makes that commitment easier is remembering that Christ fulfilled the ultimate commitment by dying on the cross for me. That's the world's all-time greatest commitment, and that's what Jesus did for you and me.

Jesus didn't have to do that, either. He didn't have to put Himself through that pain. Yet He knew that in God's plan somebody had to pay the price for our sin. God is loving and merciful, but He's also just. That means that no matter how much He loves us, He can't just look the other way when we sin. He can't pretend that our sin doesn't exist. To be able to approach God, we must be cleansed from our sin, and the only way for that to happen is if someone pays the price for it. Jesus is the only one who could pay that price, since He is the only one who is both human (and could therefore die) and divine (and thus could provide an infinitely precious sacrifice). And He did. He willingly took all sin—yours, mine, everybody's—on Himself when He was crucified. If He hadn't done that, we'd have to spend an eternity apart from Him, and Jesus loves us too much to allow that to happen.

Some Kind of Forgiveness!

Jesus told a story to illustrate exactly what His death on the cross would accomplish for you and for me. The story is sometimes called the

Parable of the Prodigal Son. This son chose to leave his family and pursue a wild lifestyle. The father, a wealthy farmer, honored his son's request to receive his share of the inheritance so he could lead his own life. The boy went out into the world to seek a great time. He partied down, drank, gambled, and squandered his money. When all his "friends" had abandoned him and he found himself alone, broke, and miserable, he finally came to his senses. A broken man, he returned to the farm—and his father forgave him and returned to him his rightful place in the family. The father even welcomed back his son by throwing a party to celebrate his return.

That's some kind of dad!

And you know what? Our heavenly Father is just like him.

Think about Christ and the sacrifice He made for us. That's something none of us could ever repay (nor should we try). I am eternally grateful for that.

Our part in being saved from eternal punishment is to confess our own sinfulness and accept what Jesus did on the cross as the payment for our sins. We have to accept Jesus into our hearts and say, "Yes, I believe that You are the Son of God and that You died for me. I can't save myself—I need the gift of Your grace that You freely offer me."

I think the simplicity of Christianity confuses some people a little. *All we have to do is trust that the Lord Jesus died for us to forgive our sins, and He will save us.*

For some people, that seems too easy. They think they have to *do* something to earn salvation and forgiveness. But that's just the point: We *can't* do anything on our own to earn God's favor. We are saved because of God's grace. It all boils down to trusting in the Lord, having faith that He is who He is and that He has done for us what He said He would do.

If we believe that, from that point on we commit ourselves to living our lives for Jesus Christ. Just as He laid down His life for us, we give our lives over to Him to allow Him to work in and through us. That's why I want to do everything I can for God's glory. I'm not doing this because I'm trying to repay Him—that's impossible—but because I'm grateful and I love Him. When you love someone, you do whatever you can to make that person happy. That's my goal, to live a life that pleases God. And that's the most important and fulfilling commitment any of us can make!

Everyday Christians

Some people think that because they are saved they can do whatever they want, no matter how evil or sinful it might be. After all, God's going to forgive them anyway. But a true Christian doesn't think like that. Can you imagine a guy saying to his sweetheart, "Darling, I love you so much that I'm going to go right out and do all kinds of evil, shameful things that will bring pain and sorrow to your heart. After all, you're my girl"? Of course not. We'd all say that guy is just using his girl; he doesn't love her at all. If he did, he'd do whatever he could to make her happy.

It's just like being a parent, something I've been blessed with myself. When I look at my son, I expect him to make mistakes at some point. I hope I can instill in him a foundation of knowing right and wrong so his mistakes won't be drastic ones. At the same time, I know he will eventually mess up. But when he does, I won't love him any less than I do now. I'll be disappointed, but I'll still have a father's love for him.

It's like that with the unconditional love God has for us. Even when we sin, He still loves us. When we make mistakes, we can ask for forgiveness, then move on. But just as I don't want to see my son make mistakes because I know he'll have to pay the consequences for his actions, God doesn't want us to suffer the consequences of our sinful actions. He loves us that much. And when we realize the love He has for us, we're motivated to live as He wants us to—every day.

When we begin to live every day for Jesus, we become everyday Christians instead of Sunday Christians. What are Sunday Christians? They are people who, when they're at church, relate everything to Christ; but during the rest of the week, they are different folks. Sunday Christians may recognize that there's a God, but they don't realize what God can do for them or fully appreciate the price Christ has paid for them by dying on the cross.

They don't understand the benefits of Jesus' words, "My peace I give you. Do not let your hearts be troubled and do not be afraid" (John 14:27).

Faith in Jesus is not a once-a-week thing. It's an everyday commitment. You get up. You thank God for letting you wake up that morning. You thank God for the many blessings that He's given you. You live your day with Christ as your constant companion. And if you slip and sin, you confess your sin as soon as you can to clear the slate with God. You feel remorse and ask God for forgiveness and help in avoiding that sin in the future.

That's part of what it means to live as an everyday Christian. And far from reducing your ability to enjoy life, it enormously increases it. I know that's what it has done for me.

So much for Sunday-only believers. But there's a second problem some people have with Christianity that I haven't yet mentioned. While some people think they can do whatever they want because they are Christians, others think that just because they put their trust in God, nothing bad will ever happen to them. When hard times come their way, these people wonder if God cares or if He even exists at all.

Yet the Bible never tells us we won't have problems. In fact, it promises that we will! (See John 15:18-20; 16:33; 2 Timothy 3:12) But we can have joy and peace in the midst of our hardships because we know that God will help us overcome our tests and temptations.

As we commit every day of our lives to God, we gain the daily joy of developing a relationship with Jesus Christ. We don't see Him merely as an insurance policy against an eternity in hell, and we don't rely on Him as a cosmic good-luck charm against difficulties in this life. Instead, we interact with Him in everything we do, and we enjoy a deep intimacy with Him in the process.

The Cowboy and His Faith

You may wonder how a member of the Dallas Cowboys can incorporate his faith into his everyday life. After all, very few things you hear about the

Cowboys have anything to do with matters of faith. Yet I have found ways, both with the team and outside the team, to grow in my faith.

Tammy and I both attend Bible Study Fellowship (BSF), an in-depth and long-term Bible study program. We're also involved in a Bible study with other Cowboy couples. And Tammy attends a women's Bible study with some of the wives of Cowboy players.

And I can say that God is working in the hearts of many of the Dallas Cowboy players!

You wouldn't know it by reading the papers, but there was a kind of a spiritual revival on the team during the 1995 season. Several players got together and started a Bible study. Some of us had deep theological discussions as the trainers taped us, and at the same time other guys would debate the meanings of Jesus' miracles and parables.

Some of us have created a community of believers, and we try to witness to other players by the way we live our lives. We've been fortunate to develop ways to worship God in the midst of an NFL team. Whether we're having a Bible study, a chapel program under the direction of chaplain John Weber, or just interacting with teammates, we can live out our commitments to God minute by minute.

While some guys have become more committed, there are Sunday Christians on the team as well. These guys proclaim that they're believers, but their lifestyles communicate something else. In the apostle Paul's words, "They claim to know God, but by their actions they deny him" (Titus 1:16). They womanize, party, lie, or cheat. Profanity is a big thing. What do you do when your teammates consistently use vulgarities? I've realized that by consciously choosing to lead my life appropriately, my example can rub off on them. In a team environment, you can't go out and single out an individual for swearing. If you do, you lose all respect and cohesiveness and that breaks down your team and your relationships. And in the end, what good have you done? Maybe the guy swears less (and maybe more), but he's still on the road to hell.

This makes living for Christ and maintaining a team spirit difficult. You have to maintain team cohesiveness, so you don't want to create friction. But as a Christian, it's hard for me to sit back and see individuals sin without confronting them.

Mostly, my role is simply to be an example. Or if I'm asked, I may tell the person, "That's wrong. I don't agree with that, and here's why. . . ."

A Faith Exercise

It's great to have members of your football team on your spiritual team as well. But there's nothing like what happens when you exercise your faith and grow spiritually at home and at church. Tammy and I have found a body of Christians in a Lutheran church just down the road from where we live, and we're grateful to God for them.

One of the things that attracted us to this church was that the people treated us as Chad and Tammy Hennings, the people, the Christian couple. They didn't treat us as Chad and Tammy Hennings, the football people—which is the way most people view us. This church saw us for the people we are behind the Cowboy image, and that was refreshing to us. It felt like family.

We needed that kind of family feeling, because a few months after Super Bowl XXX, we faced a difficult time when our son Chase became painfully and mysteriously ill.

Chase was a little over two years old when he contracted an unidentified and serious illness that landed him in the hospital for eight days. He was suddenly transformed from a happy-go-lucky, towheaded ball of energy to a listless, miserable little boy. And I mean *suddenly*. One night, he went to bed a healthy two-year-old; the next morning his legs hurt and he had a frighteningly high fever. When we took him to the hospital, the doctors poked and prodded him until I thought he couldn't stand any more. I won't be surprised if he grows up disliking anyone wearing white.

After living through my son's illness, I don't think there's any way someone can understand the depth of emotion you feel when your child is seriously ill, especially when you can't find out what's wrong.

Chase endured eight days in the hospital and about three months of tests, and the doctors still couldn't figure out what was wrong. At one time they diagnosed the difficulty as a bone infection. Another time we were told he had a virus that caused his high fever. The attempts at diagnosing and re-diagnosing went on for a couple of months as we waited for a diagnosis. For all we knew, Chase's illness could have been terminal. We just didn't know.

The doctors were trying to use a systematic approach, a process of elimination to pinpoint the problem. They'd do tests to eliminate a certain diagnosis, then move on to the next one. They ruled out cancer, leukemia, and several other diseases and still couldn't figure out what was wrong. For us, it was maddening and encouraging at the same time. No, we didn't know what was wrong, but we were eliminating some pretty horrible diseases.

It was all so frustrating. I can remember talking to the doctors about my frustration. Here we were in a country with the best medical technology in the world, with incredible advances in medicine, and we couldn't figure out what was making my son so sick. Why was he suffering? Why did he have to go through all these tests?

The doctors sympathized and admitted their own frustration. They were doing everything they could, but they were as puzzled as Tammy and I were over what was happening to Chase.

What most frustrated me about Chase's condition was that I had no control over it. I couldn't do anything to make it better. There are some things that a parent can control, but I had absolutely no control over what was happening with my son. I couldn't do anything for him. I couldn't even tell him what was wrong! Not only did I have no idea what the problem was, but he wouldn't have understood if I did. Had he been ten or twelve years old, we might rationally explain what was happening and he could gain some understanding. But Chase was two years old, and at that age, no explanation really helps. All my son could understand was that he was suffering. The situation wore down Tammy and me emotionally, mentally, and physically, while it continued to make Chase miserable.

Watching our little boy suffer was almost unbearable. It's one thing to *know* your child is sick, but it's something else to be able to *see* it. To see doctors or nurses sticking tubes up his nose or down his throat or see them constantly injecting medicine or taking blood—and watching my little guy wilt in the face of all this suffering—was almost more than we could stand.

It tore me up inside to see Chase with a fever of 105 degrees and to have to put him in a cool bath just to lower his body temperature. All the while, he's crying, wanting me to pick him up and hold him. But as much as I wanted to, I couldn't, because my body heat would have contributed to his body heat and raised his temperature even more. So we had to hold him down in the bathtub and sponge bathe him while he's struggling and crying, "Let me go."

The Diagnosis

After months of suffering, hundreds of tests and innumerable tears, we finally found out what was wrong with Chase. The doctors told us he had juvenile arthritis, and a pretty mild case of it at that. The good news is that most children grow out of juvenile arthritis. He's going to recover.

Unfortunately, we don't know how long it will take for him to fully recover. It could be months or it could be a few years. In the meantime, we'll have to help him deal with low-grade fevers and pain and stiffness in his joints.

As of the summer of 1996, our trial with Chase's illness isn't over. He is still suffering and he still has to endure mild torture, such as getting his stiff ankles massaged daily. But it is a relief to know what is wrong and to know that he's going to be OK.

At the same time, we look forward to the day when Chase is completely healthy. Right now, he can't run or jump like he used to. He was an athletic little boy, and before his illness he loved to roughhouse with Dad. We loved to wrestle. I'd take him down and let him jump on me, then I'd rough him up a little. He loved it! And so did I. I can't wait for the day when my boy is completely recovered and ready to play with his dad again the way he used to.

A Learning Experience

Every trial we go through as Christians gives us the opportunity to learn and grow in our relationship with God. Our situation with Chase's illness is a good example of this.

While we were suffering through these trying times with Chase—not knowing what was wrong with him and dedicating all of our time to being with him—we found out something very valuable about how Christians should respond to each other. Our church family showered us with support. Various families brought lunches and dinners to us. Chase received gifts of balloons, flowers, stuffed animals, and lots of other delightful things. His hospital room was jam-packed with proof that people in our congregation cared.

Through this trial, I learned new things about myself and my relationship with God. Prayer was one of those things. Here I am, a big, strong, healthy guy. I can bench-press 530 pounds. I'm one of the strongest guys on the best team in football. But despite my strength, I could do nothing for Chase—nothing except pray and be there for him.

In all the frustration and sorrow of my son's illness, I was forced to go to God as my source of strength. I didn't understand why Chase had to go through this illness and I didn't know what good could come of it. So all I could do was have faith that God would somehow use the situation to bring glory to His kingdom.

I had to reach the point where, as hard as it is to comprehend, I confessed that God loved my little boy infinitely more than Tammy and I combined could love him. When I realized that, I prayed, "Thy will be done. It's in your hands. I know you love him more than Tammy and I could ever love him."

This situation also taught me something about fear. Remember, I first learned to conquer my fears after my sophomore year in high school when I didn't wrestle. Now I was a professional football player who had gone head-to-head with the best players in the game. I had been a fighter pilot who made forty-five missions into enemy territory—and yet I was faced with a greater fear than I had ever known.

As a husband and father, your worst fear is having something go wrong with your wife or child. I can handle what happens to me. I can handle personal pain; I've experienced a lot of it. (You can't play football and not feel pain!) I've learned to fight those types of fears. But it's a completely different kind of fear when something happens to your kid or to your wife.

That's where my faith became so important to me. My wife has told me that during our time in the service when we had to be separated for so much of the time, only her faith in God kept her going. I can say the same thing about Chase's illness.

When all I could do was pray, when I was helpless to do anything else and when my worst fears began to surface, it was then I knew that I had a heavenly Father who cares as much for me as I care for Chase. And I knew that He loved Chase more than I ever could.

Yet another thing God taught me through Chase's illness was the importance of prioritizing my life so I can spend more time with Chase. I needed to adjust my life according to his needs. The more Chase needs me, the more I have to change my calendar to fit his needs.

It's difficult to see your child suffer, and it makes you wonder at times how God operates. We wondered, *Is this a teaching lesson for us, and if so, how will it benefit Chase? Or is it simply a bump along the road that we will look back on in years to come with little concern?* Questions like these come to mind among Christians who are interested in seeking God's will for their lives and who want to know how the circumstances of life mix with divine leading.

It was a helpless feeling to be unable to help my son, but it solidified my faith and my hope in God that things will work out for me and my family when we have a complete dependence on the Lord. We depended on Him before, but our ordeal with Chase has taken it to a whole new level. I could do nothing. The doctors couldn't do anything. No one could do anything for him. It was a waiting game. I had to put total dependence on God that everything was in his hands.

Throughout this ordeal, I've found a lot of comfort in John 16:33—"I have told you these things so that in me you may have peace. In this world you will have trouble. But take heart, for I have overcome the world." God has promised peace, and I rely on that promise. Because of what we've endured, I have reached a new level in my faith. I've become more dependent on the Lord. I trust that He will guide me through all things, good and bad.

Where There's God's Will . . .

Even though God guides us in all things, we sometimes have trouble discerning where He wants to lead us. Life is full of twists and turns. So how do we know which paths to follow?

I once took part in a Bible study group that studied a book titled *Experiencing God*. This book teaches Christians how to know when a choice is God's will and when it's not. Sometimes that decision is a battle between your will and God's will. As I read through *Experiencing God*, I discovered that God reveals His plans for us through prayer, meditation, circumstances, the Bible, the church, and fellow Christians. The Holy Spirit uses those areas to help us make wise choices.

When we have decisions to make, we often think we need to make them right away. Sometimes we feel pressure within ourselves to choose quickly so we can get going along a new path or stick to an old one. But I've always believed that if a decision isn't a matter of life or death, it doesn't need to be made right away. We need time to reflect on the signals God sends.

If you make Christ the lens through which you view all of life, you will not only maintain balance but you'll also be successful. You may not gain money or celebrity status, but you'll live life as God desires, and people will notice a difference in you. That's part of being committed to Christ.

When I recommitted my life to Christ in that church in England, I had no idea what God had in store for Tammy and me. We were at a decision point but had no clear direction of where to go. I just knew that the Man who hung on that old, rugged cross had hung there for me. And I knew I had to dedicate my life to His ministry of spreading the gospel.

What I didn't know was that as I committed to serve God in all I did, God was preparing Tammy and me for a remarkable opportunity in the

United States. Not as an airline pilot with a major carrier. Not as a successful farmer in Iowa. Not as a football coach at the Academy. But as a football player with America's Team, the Dallas Cowboys.

Think of it. God reached down in that little church in England and chose me to carry His love and His story of redemption into the National Football League.

All my life I had dreamed of suiting up to play in the NFL, and that dream was coming true. Yet a surprise was waiting for me. It had never dawned on me how absolutely miserable life could be for someone who was living his dream.

Welcome to an NFL training camp.

WORKOUT DRILL

1. The most important thing in Chad Hennings' life is his relationship with Jesus Christ. Can I say that about my life? Do I know for sure that Jesus is my Savior?

2. When Chad and Tammy were in England, they decided to dedicate their lives to serving God. What does that mean? How does it affect their lives every day? Have I ever made that commitment to serve God wholeheartedly? Is anything standing in my way of doing that?

3. What is so different about a commitment to God as compared to a commitment to a sport like football?

4. Chad feels that God used his post-college military commitment to get him ready spiritually for the pros. What examples have I seen recently where the life of a pro athlete has been too much for a person to handle? How can a strong faith in Jesus prevent that?

5. What is a once-a-week Christian? Am I ever guilty of keeping my faith locked up in church and never letting it out to make me a better person throughout the week? If I am, what should I do about it?

LIFE IN THE NATIONAL FOOTBALL LEAGUE CAN BE GRUELING, TIRING...SWEATY.

◄ WELCOME TO THE NFL ►

TOUGH GAME, TOUGH GUYS, AND A RETIRED AIR FORCE CAPTAIN

No champion has ever achieved his goal without showing more dedication than the next person; making more sacrifices than the next person; working harder than the next person; training and conditioning himself more than the next person; studying more than the next person; enjoying his final goal more than the next person.

DOAK WALKER

I've got some advice for you if anyone ever asks you to report to an NFL training camp.

Say "no."

Or at least if you say "yes," make sure you have a chance to get yourself in really good shape before you set foot in camp.

Although I'm glad I didn't say "no" to the Cowboys when my opportunity came, I sure wish I had been better prepared when I first stepped out of the locker room at our training facility and attempted to show Jimmy Johnson what a wise choice he had made in keeping me.

When I tell you how things went at training camp my first year, I want you to know that I'm not complaining. I have nothing to complain about. Yet there's value in knowing what it takes to get physically and mentally ready for an NFL season and the difficulty in doing so. Especially when you're wrong about how ready you really are.

Starting Over

After I returned to England following my Cowboy tryout, Tammy and I had a month to pack, move to the United States, set up housekeeping, and get ready for training camp. Here I was, an Air Force captain who had been sitting in the cockpit of jet fighters for the previous few years, and I was about to bang heads with some extremely tough men who had been pumping iron and manhandling tackling dummies the whole time I had been operating a joy stick.

This could be . . . interesting.

Researchers have rated how different kinds of stress affect a person's work record. Among the two stresses that affect a person the most are a change in occupation and moving to a new location. Not many rookies in the NFL have to change from some other job to football, because most of them have just spent the previous four or five years playing collegiate ball. And not many rookies have to move from a foreign country to begin their careers. If the experts were right about those stress factors, I would be operating under a tremendous amount of stress at my first Cowboys' training camp.

They were right. By the time I got to training camp after rushing to get out of the Air Force, making a transatlantic move, and helping Tammy get us settled, I was burned out mentally and physically. I was completely drained.

This is where all those years of learning about commitment paid off for me. Ever since my earliest years on the farm, I had been instructed to stick to the task, to gut it out even when things got tough. Again, I would be tested on my commitment. As I began, I knew I had to stay focused, avoid distractions, and not let anything diminish my commitment if I were to have a prayer of making the Dallas Cowboys.

Welcome to Training Camp

The Cowboys hold training camp at St. Edwards' University in Austin, Texas, and it lasts for six weeks. When I first joined the team, our coach was Jimmy Johnson, known for his militaristic approach to coaching. As someone who knows about military training, I can verify the accuracy of those reports. Coach Johnson made things extremely tough.

Then there were some things even Jimmy Johnson had no control over. Like the weather. I was accustomed to England's weather, with high temperatures around sixty-five degrees, and I was training in south Texas where it was 110 degrees.

Remember back in chapter 3 when I talked about cramping because of the heat at basic training in Colorado Springs? Well, it was that and worse—much worse—at the Cowboys' training camp. Many times I would become so dehydrated that the trainers had to stick an IV in my arm to give me fluids. I suffered this dehydration for the first time after the first day of camp. That night, Tammy and I went out to eat, and Tammy had to drive because I could barely move. When we got to the restaurant, my body started locking up. I was cramping everywhere. I had abdomen and upper-body cramps—I even had forehead cramps!

I had to return to training camp to get an IV stuck in my arm. I sat there thinking, *Oh, man. This is going to be a long training camp.* The doctor who treated me said, "You're going to be sore tomorrow like you've never been sore before." He explained to me that the type of cramping I suffered is like going through an intense workout, and the soreness would result.

Weight loss was another physical problem I faced at training camp. I'd lose ten pounds just in morning practice. At the time, I wasn't disciplined and knowledgeable enough about my personal physiology to know how to prevent those kinds of problems. Later, I learned that I had to drink two gallons of water a day just to stay hydrated. Plus I had to take supplements such as phosphates to restore nutrients that had been depleted through such vigorous exercise. But I didn't know about this stuff during my first camp, and I paid the price.

After that first day ends, you know what happens next: the second day. Sore as I was, I had to return to camp the next day. And the next. And the next. I struggled through that entire training camp, just hoping I could survive.

Then to add to the physical torment I was already suffering, I got hurt during my first exhibition game. We played that game on artificial turf, and I hadn't set foot on that stuff since college. So during the game, I landed on my foot wrong and severely sprained my big toe. So now, in addition to having sore muscles, I couldn't push off. There I was, trying to show the coaching staff what I could do, and I had this big, bad, swollen, black-and-blue turf toe that kept me from pushing off. It was a big-time gut check for me.

As the days passed, the toe wouldn't heal. I kept aggravating the injury, but I never took any time off. For one thing, I wanted to impress the coaches. For another, the Cowboys had a couple of defensive linemen who were holding out for better contracts, so the Cowboys needed me. I had to keep playing.

At times during that first summer I had my doubts about whether I could do this. Yes, I knew that if God wanted me to be a member of the Dallas Cowboys—and with the way events had transpired, I believed He did—He'd get me on the team. But I knew that I still had to perform well to get the staff's attention.

That's a lesson I had learned. God supplies the plan of action for us, but it's up to us to follow that plan. Sometimes it's not easy, and it's tougher at times to follow God's plan than to take another pathway. But I was here, and I knew He had put me here. Now it was up to me.

Still, there were times when I questioned the sanity of the whole thing. I'd ask myself, "Is it ever going to get any easier?" Training for professional football was pure torture. I thought I had been in pretty good shape when I arrived at camp, but nothing could prepare someone mentally or physically for what I was enduring. I really doubted my chances.

One of the reasons I faced these doubts was that I hadn't talked with anybody about what to expect. I had been involved so heavily in overseas work and with my flight training that I didn't have a chance to prepare myself for the rigors of professional football. Of course, I had spent four summers at the Air Force Academy going through training camp, but this was different. Professional football training camp was more physical and more intense than our workout at the Air Force Academy. In college, the NCAA regulates the amount of time you can do certain things. It says you have to build your way up gradually. When you get to the NFL, you're on the spot as soon they throw the gates open.

Every day of training camp I'd go to my dorm room after practice, lay on my bed, and pray, "God help me." I received much of that help through my own personal Bible study and daily devotional time. I'd do that every morning. I knew that if I was going to keep my commitment to football, it was vital that I keep my commitment to God strong. He is my power source, and I knew I couldn't afford a blackout.

Meanwhile, Back at the Ranch

While I was struggling to make a go of it in training camp, Tammy was encountering culture shock of her own. She had to settle into a new home, a new neighborhood, and a new routine.

And, really, we were still just getting to know each other. We'd been married only two years, and I'd been gone for half of that with my military obligations. During those years I'd often be on a deployment mission, and Tammy would be left in England by herself. She didn't know many people and was separated from her support group by an ocean and half a continent. There were many days of loneliness that Tammy spent in deep thought and prayer.

When I got my opportunity to play for the Cowboys, it was a stressful time for Tammy, too. She was excited about what was happening to me, but she was also apprehensive about the move and the career change.

Now we'd made the big move back to the United States, and we were apart again. I was down at camp in Austin, and Tammy was up in Dallas in an apartment. She must have felt like, "Here we go again!"

(In terms of separation, Tammy and I have found that my playing in the NFL is much better than when I was in the Air Force. You can plan on training camp and know when it's coming and how long it will last. In the Air Force, I never knew from one week to the next where I'd be sent or how long I'd stay there.)

A wife's commitment to her husband's profession is so crucial. It's important to anybody, be it in the world of business or retail or whatever. Tammy is my support, and any time that I feel down or question certain things, she's there for me. Her commitment to my serving in the Air Force had to be at least as strong as mine. And when I was at training camp for the Cowboys, I was asking her to do the same thing.

And she came through. She was such an encouragement to me, especially when I thought my body might break down. She never said, "quit feeling sorry for yourself" or anything like that. She was always very positive. She said, "You're here for a purpose. God wants you here." That's nice to hear when you're hurting in places you forgot you had.

Fortunately, training camp eventually gives way to the regular season, and the dedication and commitment shown by players and family alike finally pay off. The real fun begins as we match wits and muscles with a new opponent each weekend for the next seventeen weeks.

Put Me In, Coach!

When you're the new guy on the block, you don't expect to play right away. But of course, that doesn't stop you from hoping you might. And to better your chances, you have to carve out a niche for yourself.

I had survived training camp and my rookie season had finally started. I was eager to play, but after I had been inactive for the first six games, I began to wonder, *What can I do?*

I had come out of college as the Outland Trophy winner, and my own perception was that despite the layoff, I should be able to pick up right where I had left off. But in reality, I had to relearn everything. I mentioned doing countless drills, and as I did, I tried to reteach myself how to make the moves naturally.

The encouraging part of my first season with the Cowboys was that I had made the team and become part of the organization. I was continuing to put on physical size and strength and I was doing all the things the coaches wanted.

But my frustration grew as I tried to reestablish myself as a football player, and I felt doubly frustrated because I wasn't seeing the fruit of my hard work—I wasn't playing at all. In fact, I didn't dress for the first five games of the season, then I dressed for the sixth game but didn't play.

Now I realize that in general the NFL coaches don't like to play rookies because their first year is supposed to be a learning period. A rookie might start out of necessity or if they're really outstanding. But I had been away from the game for four years, and I had a lot to learn and relearn.

No doubt I had some unrealistic expectations for my rookie year. I believed that I was going to come in and contribute right off the bat. I did the workout, had a good training camp, and possessed all the physical characteristics they were looking for. But translating that physical talent into football skills can be tough, especially for a guy who was so rusty from having taken four years away from football.

The second obstacle to earning playing time was team depth at my position. It was a numbers game, really, and I was the low guy on the totem pole. The Cowboys were three-deep at every position, including defensive tackle. We had Russell Maryland, Tony Casillas, Jimmie Jones, Leon Lett, and Danny Noonan. Obviously, it would be tough for me to break into the rotation.

I didn't fault Coach Johnson for my lack of playing time. He was doing what he thought would win football games, and I respected that. But I wanted to be a part of the picture, and my only option as a defensive lineman on a team stacked with defensive linemen, was to contribute on special teams.

One Monday I approached Coach Johnson and said, "Coach, what would it take for me to get on special teams? Do I have to run a 4.5, 4.6 forty, or what?" I think he respected that. I must have struck a chord with him, because the next day he told me that special-teams coach Joe Avezzano wanted to talk to me about some special-teams assignments.

The next Sunday I had my pro football debut against the Detroit Lions. It was incredibly exciting for me because I finally felt as if I were contributing on a National Football League team. Standing on the sidelines all those weeks didn't give me the feeling I was part of the team. But now I would be a player, one of the guys. That day, it felt like I was putting on pads for the first time. Even though I had gone through training camp and all the practices, this was different. I *knew* I was going to play. The butterflies were playing loop-the-loop inside my stomach.

On that first kickoff, I was in the game. I was playing in the NFL! I remember running downfield with reckless abandon. I felt like screaming my head off. Immediately, my teammates on the kickoff-coverage team gave me the nickname Wedgebuster. I was the middle guy and given the task of moving down the field and wreaking havoc.

I ended up making three tackles in my first game and I should have had two more. On one play my excitement got the best of me and I ended up running right past the guy returning the ball! It was Mel Gray, one of the top kickoff-return specialists in the game.

That was my first real taste of the NFL. After one game, I knew I could succeed in this league. My next step was to work my way into the rotation as a defensive tackle. The problem with that was that the Cowboys had me listed as a defensive end, a position I had never played. I had played tackle during my last three years in college, and I was like a fish out of water at defensive end. The techniques of playing end are different than those at tackle. Basically, it's working in free space versus playing in confined quarters with two or more guys hitting you from different directions (which is more my kind of football!).

Fortunately for me, Coach Johnson is known as a good judge of football talent. He realized I was playing out of position at end. Midway through the season, he came up to me and said, "I know we put you in a difficult position at defensive end, when you're a defensive tackle. Just by watching you, I can see you're a defensive tackle."

I started practicing as a defensive tackle and before long I was actually getting some playing time, spelling players at both tackle and end. By the time of the Super Bowl, I was still playing special teams, but I was also playing on the line.

Despite the lack of playing time, I got a lot out of my first year in the NFL, mostly because I learned a lot about technique. It didn't take me long to realize this about technique in the NFL: You have to have it. Good athletic ability, strength, and size will get you only so far. No matter how big and strong and athletic you are, you have to learn technique. Being a good technician gives you longevity in the league.

I began to feel comfortable in different stances at different positions. I learned what the defensive end does as well as the defensive tackle. All these steps were growing opportunities that helped me in the long-run because I was learning the game.

That brings me back to a subject we touched on earlier: flexibility. When I look at my first year in the NFL, I realize how important it was for me to understand this concept. I had to be flexible from the first game of the year simply because I wasn't playing. I had to maintain an attitude of flexibility in order to be ready when they called my name. I had to keep my mind and body sharp and continue to practice at a high level, even when it didn't pay immediate dividends.

I also had to be flexible in order to adjust to my change in position. While defensive end isn't my natural position, I had to be flexible and learn to play that spot in order to fulfill my commitment to my team. And I had to be flexible as I was learning to play on special teams.

It's the same way with game plans. If you're in a game and your opponent throws a surprise at you, you have to be able to adapt on the run.

That first season was a season of adjustments for me, that's for sure. Adjusting to playing football again. Adjusting to a new system. Adjusting to different positions. Adjusting to the National Football League. But, oh my, was it worth it!

On the Field

Let me take you down on the field with me to see what a game in the NFL is all about. It's an exciting challenge that requires a commitment to being tough both physically and mentally.

Someone has just finished singing the national anthem and the teams have completed warmups. We're standing anxiously on our sideline, looking across the field at our opponents and thinking about what it will take to stop them. I'm straining my eyes to find the numbers of the guys I'll line up against in just a couple of minutes. When I see them, I try to size them up physically.

Finally it's time for the game to begin. If the Cowboys have the ball first, we defenders have to anxiously wait a little longer, pacing the sideline, eager to get into the action. Then at last, it's our turn. With the energy of pent-up emotions, we charge onto the field. It's a bit chaotic as the offensive and defensive teams switch places and forty-four men run to their positions. When everyone gets lined up, there's a strong feeling of anticipation. I stand across the line from the offensive linemen, feeling a little nervous and apprehensive. This stays with me until the center makes the snap, when my teammates and I come flying off the ball.

As a defensive lineman, I am prepared to take new ground. Our opponents have what we want—the ball. And we have what they want—the goal line behind us. It makes for an intense struggle.

As Dallas Cowboy defenders, we have a certain way we play defense. Our goal is to come off the ball as hard as we can and hit the offensive linemen in a controlled collision. We want to get our hands on the offensive lineman while figuring out if the opponent will run or pass.

Right after we break the huddle, our defensive captains call out a specific defense. We break, look up, and our opponents are setting their positions. As we wait, we decide which technique to use: shading outside the guard, inside the guard, or outside the center.

As we're in our defensive stance, just before the snap of the ball which begins the chaos that ensues at the line of scrimmage in the NFL, we try to observe anything that might give us an advantage. We're looking down, but we can see the center's stance, observe the position of his hands, and watch the position of the quarterback's hands underneath the center. If I'm lined up with the offensive guard, I'm looking in front of him to see if he's "sitting light." In other words, I look to see if his heels are up or down, or if there's a lot of pressure on his fingers. Those signs help me predict whether he'll come off the ball straight or back up to pass block.

I also look at the opponents' pass splits—the amount of distance between their feet—to see if the play will be a run or a pass. And I look at the backfield set to see how many backs and receivers are in the upcoming play. I also look at how they line up and any checks or adjustments that they make.

I have to process all these elements before I get down in my stance. When I do, I'm looking for my opponent's tendencies. If he's sitting back, I know it's going to be a pass, some sort of draw, or a pulling play. Because I want to get a good jump off the ball, I adjust my stance accordingly. If I notice that he's leaning forward—and I can tell that if I see that he's heavy on his fingers and if his heels are up—I know the offense is planning a running play. I'll tee off on my man, and he'll try to do the same to me. My goal is to negate his energy, smack him hard, and stand him up. We want to control our opponent. If we can control him by getting him twisted in any manner, even if he simply turns his shoulder pads, he's going to have less opportunity to tee off on us.

Defensive linemen are usually going against guys who weigh more than 300 pounds, and most of us are 290 pounds or lighter. On top of that, NFL offensive linemen aren't just big, they're very athletic. It's amazing to me that men that big can move as well as they do. When I came into the league I was told about the athletic abilities of the offensive linemen, but there's really nothing that can prepare you to see a 330-pound man who can move like that. You have to experience it to understand it.

My position always gets double-teamed, which is much tougher to handle. It's like running into a small Volkswagen and knowing that you've got to get past it. When I'm double-teamed, I'm pushing on one guy and trying to get around him while fighting off the second guy. Sometimes there's even a third guy if the center backs out and hits you. It's like running the gauntlet.

Every play is basically a little street fight. It's five to seven seconds of intense, all-out physical contact, and then it's over for thirty to forty-five seconds. You catch your breath, march back up to the line, and do it all over again.

Life on the Line

Questionable calls by officials can be maddening, but there's something else that can make NFL life tough. Sometimes players on opposing teams look for ways to cause problems on the field. For instance, you don't want to be standing around a pileup against certain individuals. If you make yourself too available, they'll hit you after the play has ended. Other players will punch. During a game, even after the play is whistled dead, you always have to be alert. It's like keeping your head on a swivel the whole time.

Some offensive players have done things to me with the intent of injuring me. When that happens, I have to take steps to remedy the situation. Now, it's not in my nature to fight. In fact, you'd have to do something pretty outrageous to get me to fight. Besides, I've learned that fighting isn't just a bad witness, it's a waste of energy, something you need to make good use of during the game.

I've realized something about being a Christian playing a violent—and, unfortunately, sometimes dirty—game: God doesn't require me to be a wimp or to allow people to try to injure me. God wants me to compete and be aggressive. And part of being aggressive is taking steps to prevent people from intentionally hurting me.

Yet the biggest offense I have noticed in the NFL isn't cheap shots, but that offensive linemen are routinely guilty of holding. It's just a fact of the game. Therefore defensive linemen have to do certain things to try to negate the holding. I accept holding as a part of the game, but at the same time I look for ways to counteract it.

One reason offensive linemen do this is because the game has evolved so much. People want to see offenses score a lot of points. Techniques on both sides of the ball have had to change with the fans' increasing expectations, and holding is part of that change. I don't hold any grudges against offensive linemen because of it; they're doing what they have to do to be successful. But it sure makes the game more physical.

Hard hits are also a part of the game, and sometimes players get hurt because of them. In 1995, the NFL decided to crack down on excessively hard hits on quarterbacks. That was meant to send a signal to all defensive players that when you tackle the quarterback, you shouldn't try to hurt him. For me, that hasn't been much of a problem because I don't consciously try to hurt anyone. Like all defensive players, I want to solidly hit quarterbacks to make them remember me and think twice about sitting in the pocket, but I'd never try to hurt anyone. I do nothing flagrant, nothing dirty.

With all the possible animosity that could be floating back and forth across the line, you'd think the line of scrimmage would be the scene of some brutal verbal battles. But I've found that when we get up to the line, we're all too busy to worry about trash talk. When we get into formation and stand across the line from our opponents, several things are happening. For one thing, we're talking to each other along our side of the line of scrimmage. We're yelling things like, "Hey, I see a certain lineup," or "They're unbalanced to the right!" or "I see this over here. How 'bout you?" "Yeah, I got it."

On the other side, the offensive linemen are making their calls, so there's a lot of communication going on. But there's not too much give-and-take across the line from opponent to opponent.

For me, trash talk is a waste of energy. The amount of energy that requires can be better used for the next few plays. Just like nervousness before the game can sap my energy, so can useless communication during a game. If I say anything, I try to praise my opponents. I do that because I realize it's not a good idea to give your opponent any further motivation against you.

Playing with Pain

Another reality of life in the NFL is living with pain. What else can you expect when three hundred-pound guys smash into you with everything they have?

One of my worst times for playing with pain came in our November 12, 1995 game against the San Francisco 49ers. I sprained the medial collateral ligament in my right knee when I was hit with a chopblock. No penalty was called on the chopblock, even though we considered it a flagrant hit. The team sent a protest of that play to the league office, but nothing ever came of it.

I ended up playing the rest of that series before coming out and telling team trainer Kevin O'Neill and the team orthopedic doctor Robert VanDemeer that my knee felt a little loose.

VanDemeer said, "Okay, there's not much we can do for you here right now. Do you think you can still play?" I said, "Yes." So he stuck a neoprene sleeve with a brace on my knee, and I played the rest of the game. There was more than half the game still to go and I didn't want to come out. At this point in the season, I was starting for the Cowboys, and I wanted to make sure I could continue to contribute.

Coming back from that injury was my biggest challenge of the 1995 season. Our next opponent was the Raiders, and with the help of the team trainers I was able to make it back and play. I really had to. One of our defensive tackles had received a suspension and another was on the injured list with a sprained MCL he suffered in a game with Atlanta two weeks before I was hurt, so we didn't have any defensive tackles to spare. It was time to suck it up and go out on the field. I'm glad I did, because I had one of my best games that day.

That's what commitment is all about. It means taking the challenge and succeeding despite the obstacles. Sometimes it means participating when you're not at your best and doing what you can to contribute.

As I look toward the 1996 season, I can say with gratitude that I've not missed any games in my career because of injury. But I've faced plenty of times when I didn't feel like going out there and pounding it out with the giants of the gridiron.

I remember a game with Atlanta during my rookie year. I had been bitten big-time by the influenza bug. I was throwing up and I had diarrhea right up until game time. I mean, I was floating.

I remember coming off the field from running a sixty-yard sprint for kickoff coverage on the special-teams unit. I returned to the bench and sucked on oxygen for two minutes just to keep from passing out. But I kept going, because that's what they pay me to do.

In situations like that, I depend on the power of prayer. I say, "God, if You want me to play, grant me the strength to go out and to do my best." Then I stay focused. I try not to think "I'm sick" or "My leg hurts." I focus on the positive, not the negative.

Sometimes the pain has nothing to do with being ill or trying to manhandle a three hundred-pound behemoth. For example, at Texas Stadium, the turf can cause some nasty carpet burns. It's flat turf, but it's sticky in some places. When you're right in the middle of the painted star on the field, you don't want to go down because that's where you get the worst burns.

You also have to watch out for getting a finger caught in the helmet or the shoulder pads of your opponent. I've broken a couple of fingers doing that, and it's one of the most painful injuries you can get.

Early in a game, we are fresh and raring to go and we don't feel the pain as much. Our intensity and focus are so great that we don't notice injuries too much in the first quarter. But toward the second, third, and fourth quarters, the old body begins to get tired.

Or hot. In Texas and some of the other hot spots in the league, a September game-time temperature might be 90 to 100 degrees. But on the field, it might be 110 to 130 degrees. Then the problem is dehydration. When it's that hot, we drink a lot of water. Some guys have to go back and get an IV at halftime just to stay saturated and to keep their fluid levels high enough. We also have coolers that blow misty air on us on the sidelines, and we sometimes grab the oxygen masks and suck oxygen.

All of these things can make it tough out there on the field.

Sometimes as a game progresses, the TV sports commentators will mention that the defense has been on the field for a long time. When it's hot and you've battled those huge offensive linemen all day, the fourth quarter can seem to take forever. If the opposing offense drives against you for a long time and you're trying to stop them late in the final quarter, you feel a lot of pressure. And when you're on the field for ten to twelve consecutive plays during that long drive, you're at a true commitment checkpoint. You feel physically drained. At times you think you can't make it back to the huddle for the next play. That's when you reach down deep and find that little extra something to keep you going.

You'll notice that late in many games, teams will go to a hurry-up, no-huddle offense. I'll tell you the truth—those are killers for the defense. It's bang, bang, bang. You don't even have time to substitute. Even with the tackle rotation that we used in the 1995 season—in which three of us play two positions and rotate in and out during the drive—it's not easy. We've each played forty-five downs or so, and two of us are trying to hold our ground while the other is out trying to catch his breath. By the end, all three of us are worn out.

The Days After

If we've played in Dallas, I drive myself home after the game. At this point I don't feel as terrible as I'm going to feel on Monday or especially on Tuesday.

But first I have to get through the night. Sometimes when I come home after a game, I can't sleep the whole night. Sometimes that happens because I'm on a rush from the game; other times, my body has a hard time settling down because of all the activity. It's not unusual for me to stay up all night after games either watching television or replaying the games in my mind.

If I do get some sleep, the next morning when I try to get out of bed I think that only an act of God will help. Not only am I still exhausted and aching from head to toe, I face dehydration, especially on days after games played in intense heat. If I feel this way, I have to work on being rehydrated. That means drinking fluids until I think I can't take another drink.

On Mondays we work out. Although it sounds like torture, the best thing we can do for ourselves is to get some physical activity. This helps us to begin working through our soreness. By running, riding exercise bikes, and lifting weights, we flush a lot of the toxins out of our systems and that helps the soreness to pass.

Besides my Monday workout, I might also take a cold plunge. It's the same principle the Scandinavians use when they jump in the snow after a warm jacuzzi. First, I get into a cold plunge, in which the water is fifty to fifty-two degrees. Then I move to a warm jacuzzi. I spend thirty seconds in each one, moving back and forth three or four times.

Also on Mondays, we begin to treat things like muscle bruises and other aches and pains. The day after a game, there are always a ton of guys in the training room getting treated with ice packs, electronic muscle-stimulation units, heat, and massages.

Monday is rehab day, but we also begin focusing on the next week, which means looking at films and talking about our upcoming opponent.

Tuesday is technically our day off, but I go in and lift weights. I generally lift three days a week. On two of those days I focus on upper-body strength and on the other day I concentrate on my legs and lower body. During the season our workouts are based on maintaining our strength, not necessarily gaining weight or strength.

On Wednesday morning, it's still a little rough to get out of bed and get going. But by afternoon, I generally feel better. In the NFL, pain or lack of it is a relative thing. Football players are used to soreness and to the punishment that our bodies take—we live with pain every day. So while I may feel fine by Wednesday afternoon, another player might still be sore from Sunday's game.

Wednesday and Thursday are our heavy physical days of practice. On those mornings I try to get to the practice facility in Irving by 7:45. I lift weights before the team gets together to start preparing for Sunday. We'll have special-teams meetings and position meetings in which the coaches go over the scouting reports from our next opponent, talk about our game plan, and evaluate film. At 11:00 A.M. we take a break and then walk through the issues we just talked about.

On our two heavy workout days, we hit the lunch line at about noon. After eating, we get taped, get treatment from the trainers, finish up our weightlifting, and prepare for practice. From 1:00-1:30 P.M. we attend meetings for another review of game films. At about 1:45 P.M. we're out on the field in full pads, ready to go. For the next two hours, we go at it in practice.

During this time, we do individual drills. We practice reading offensive blocks and work on tackling techniques. We don't take each other to the ground, but we're still very physical.

Then we turn to team drills. We use the scouting reports to imitate what our opponents will do in our next game. For example, if we're going to play the Dolphins that week, our offense will run the Miami offense so our defense can learn to defend against it. Then we reverse roles. We look at the opposing defense that's scripted on a card. The coaches will draw up a particular play and we line up in the appropriate defense at our position. We run whatever the coaches want—it may be to blitz a certain gap or play a technique a certain way. So we get extra practice time working our techniques, but in our opponent's defenses.

We have to be careful as we do this. For instance, we don't tackle the running back and we don't touch the quarterback. It's physical play on the line between offense and defense, that's for sure. But we don't hit the skill players (as they are called).

One of the great things in my career with the Cowboys is that every day in practice I get to go up against some of the best players in the NFL. When someone asks me who are the toughest guys to play against, I think I surprise him when I say they're the guys I face every day in practice. Our offensive line is phenomenal. The guys are huge. Nate Newton is 6' 3" and weighs 320 pounds. Larry Allen is the same height and tips the scales at 325. Ray Donaldson is a little guy at 300 pounds, and Mark Tuinei goes 6' 5" and 305 pounds.

So when practice ends at 4:00 P.M. on Wednesday and Thursday, you can see why I'm more than ready to call it a day.

When the Season Ends

When the final buzzer sounds and the football season is put to rest for another year, I don't look at the off-season as a vacation from football. Although I don't have to report to practice every day like I do from July through January, I feel strongly that I have to continue to work out. It's all part of my commitment to the Cowboys. They pay me and they expect me to contribute to another championship team in the year to come. If I don't do that, I'm taking their money under false pretenses.

Between the end of the season (which fortunately for us has often meant the end of January) and March 1, I take some time to let my body heal from the season. This is important, because as you've seen, football players take quite a beating. Since I'm going to push my body hard for the next eleven months, this February hiatus gives everything a chance to recuperate.

This also gives me time to concentrate on my family. Tammy, Chase, and I do some traveling during this time; we often visit our families in Iowa and Colorado. In February, I don't touch a weight. I don't do any physical activity. I'm the ultimate couch potato.

But on March 1, I start getting ready for the season. Along with some of my teammates, I lift weights four days a week. On the fifth day (as well as on other days occasionally) we do some sort of physical activity, such as playing basketball. My goal in March is to begin bulking up, trying to increase my strength and weight to where they should be. From March 1 until camp begins, I am dedicated to my workouts.

During this time, Tammy, Chase, and I might still take family vacations, but I do not want to be gone too long from the gym. I'm committed to getting better, so I have to keep up my schedule. If we want to take a long weekend, we'll leave on a Thursday. But when I come back I adjust my schedule to get in the number of workouts that I need. I figure that if I lose a couple of workouts, I've cheated myself and my teammates. I don't want to do that. It's not fair to me and it's not fair to my team.

Many guys don't dedicate themselves to off-season training, but that doesn't change what I do. My commitment to the Cowboys says, "They're going to pay me no matter what, but I'm going to work out. I'm committed to doing this even though nobody's holding a gun to my head."

I start running in April while I continue to bulk up. At the end of April, right after the draft, we have quarterback school and mini-camps. The new draftees and free agents come in for a couple of days. The veterans continue to work together for a week after the rookies leave, which brings us up to the first week in May.

In May, I continue to hit the weights hard, still trying to bulk up to my playing weight. During the first week of June, we have a three-day quarterback school. By this time everybody's back in the Dallas area and the rookies are out of school or have graduated. Later, we have a three-day mini-camp where we do our running tests and some of our other lifting tests. This gives the coaches a good idea of their player resources when our training camp opens mid-July in Austin.

Which brings us back to where we started this chapter: In the hot Texas sun, ready to commit the next several months to the pursuit of excellence . . . and another run at the Super Bowl.

WORKOUT DRILL

1. What has been the most stressful thing I've faced in the past few months? Chad Hennings had to sign out of the military, move himself and Tammy from England to Texas, and go to his first NFL training camp. What character traits were most helpful to him? Which of those characteristics would help me in my stressful times?

2. As Chad faced training camp, Tammy had to make some incredible adjustments and, at the same time, support Chad's efforts. How does that relate to me and how I interact with my family members who are helping me reach my goals?

3. Pro football players and other athletes of world-class ability make their game look so easy. What has Chad's experience shown me about how difficult their task really is? What is the hardest thing I've ever had to do, whether it was in school, in sports, or in service for God? How did I survive it, and what lessons did I learn?

4. What is one of my primary goals in life? Am I as committed to reaching that goal as Chad Hennings is to becoming the best player he can be for the Cowboys? What does Chad's off-season workout dedication teach me about reaching my goals?

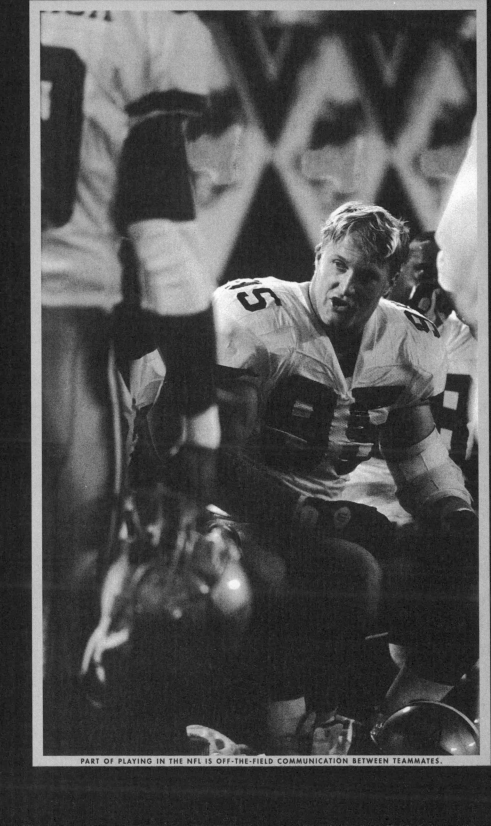

PART OF PLAYING IN THE NFL IS OFF-THE-FIELD COMMUNICATION BETWEEN TEAMMATES.

CHAPTER EIGHT

BEING A DALLAS COWBOY

MAMAS, LET YOUR BABIES GROW UP TO BE COWBOYS

I use the word hungry to describe what I mean when I talk about desire.
Being hungry provides you with the physical and mental energies necessary for
success. The sacrifices that are necessary become easier when one places
a goal or objective at a high level.

ARA PARSEGHIAN

The Dallas Cowboys have been hungry for as long as they've been in existence. Hungry for success. Hungry for the honor that comes with being the best at something. More than almost any other sports franchise in America, the Cowboys have satisfied that hunger, feasting on the success of five Super Bowl championships.

I must admit that not everything every Dallas Cowboy has done in the bright lights of public notice has been admirable. But that does not take anything away from the men who have been so influential over the thirty-plus years that the team has been in the NFL.

When I was growing up, I was one of those kids who knew and loved the Dallas Cowboys. The players I knew about and looked up to were not only outstanding players, but outstanding people. Quarterback Roger Staubach and defensive tackle Bob Lilly were among those Cowboys who not only played well, but were good people off the field. Staubach and Lilly were role models to me. They were good family men, good people, and good Christians.

Yet Roger Staubach and Bob Lilly are only two of many reasons why, in my book, Dallas has always been America's Team.

Imagine what it means to me to be a member of this team. First, I have the opportunity to meet some of those great players from another era—my childhood heroes. And second, I'm part of this winning tradition. My status as a Dallas Cowboy is a little like a "Hail Mary" pass in football. If the team that throws that pass comes up with a completion, they've accomplished an unlikely feat. From that moment on, you can only look back on that play and say, "Wow! I can't believe it!"

I'm proud to be a Cowboy and I'd like to give you a short history lesson about my team. Just as I value my family heritage—remember, the Hennings clan has lived in the same house for more than a century—so I value the heritage of the Dallas Cowboys. I thoroughly enjoy telling the story of how the team got to be such a proud franchise.

From Landry to Today

As most fans know, Tom Landry was the only head coach the team ever had until Jimmy Johnson took over in 1989. In 1960, when Clint Murchison, Jr. and Bedford Wayne were awarded a new NFL franchise, they hired Landry, who until then had been an assistant coach for the New York Giants.

Six months after the franchise was formed, the team's thirty-six veterans and a collection of rookies reported to training camp and became the Dallas Cowboys. As happens to most expansion teams, the Cowboys performed miserably that first season, ending the year at 0-11-1. Yet there were signs of life. Besides the resourceful Landry, the Cowboys had quarterback Don Meredith, a ray of hope for the future.

The 1961 season opened with great expectations, as the Cowboys rolled out to a 3-1 record—but then reality hit. The team finished 4-9-1 that year, but was beginning to accumulate more talent, including halfback Don Perkins and defensive tackle Bob Lilly.

The Cowboys continued to make progress, but it wasn't until 1966 that the team began to be recognized as a powerhouse in the NFL. Some teams go for decades without the success that Dallas enjoyed over the next several seasons. Between 1966 and 1971, the Cowboys won their conference each year. And in 1971, the team made its first appearance in the Super Bowl. In the next twenty-five years, the Cowboys would play in the Big Game a remarkable eight times.

Most of what the Cowboys have accomplished came under Landry, one of the true NFL coaching legends. By the time Landry hung up his clipboard for the last time in 1988, he had won 270 games and lost 178 as the Cowboys' head coach.

A New Era of Champions

When I joined the Cowboys in 1992, the team had been through a series of down years, yet it was clearly on the rise again. In Landry's last year and Johnson's first, the teams combined for a 4-28 record. The proud Cowboys were struggling. But in 1991, the team made the playoffs for the first time since 1985 and seemed ready to return to its former glory.

One look at the Cowboys' accomplishments during my first four years with the team shows how fortunate I was to arrive when I did. We made the playoffs and played in the National Football Conference championship game each year, winning the Super Bowl three times. Cowboy pride is back, and I'm extremely honored to be a part of it.

I can still remember the first time I put on a Dallas Cowboys uniform. It was a humbling experience, because I thought of all the guys who had run through that tunnel leading into Texas Stadium. I had grown up watching Cowboys' Super Bowl highlights of the early '70s. I knew about legendary players such as Staubach, Lilly, Meredith, Drew Pearson, Tony Dorsett, Pat Donovan, Randy White, Lee Roy Jordan, and Mel Renfro (just to name a few). I knew about the fame of the Dallas Cowboy cheerleaders. And I knew how crazy the people of Dallas were about their team.

I also remember another time when the Cowboy mystique overwhelmed me. Tammy and I were attending an awards presentation before we went to my first training camp. The team was making it quite an affair, complete with bands. This was supposed to be the big season when we would return to the playoffs. I remember sitting in the press box after the awards ceremony, looking out on the field, and saying, "I'm actually going to be playing out there." It took my breath away.

The first time I ran out on the field for a game, I had a tremendous case of nervous jitters. I had to get back to myself, downplay everything, and try to maintain a level emotional tone. I had to keep it all in control so that I wouldn't expend volumes of nervous energy. It was definitely an awesome, humbling experience.

There simply is a certain mystique or aura about this team. When the Dallas Cowboys take the field, they believe they're going to win. I don't think they ever lost that attitude, even during the down years when the team had to retool and rebuild. Even then, the Cowboys went on the field knowing they could win. And they kept plugging away until it happened. That's where commitment, persistence, and patience came in.

Although there's nothing about the team now that resembles the one that first became known as America's Team in the '70s—it has new owners, new management, new coaches, new players—yet that same attitude is still there. It hasn't changed at all.

Maybe a partial explanation for this is that the team is headquartered in Texas, where self-confidence and pride have never been in short supply. Remember, Texas was once a country in its own right before it joined the Union. And there's that feeling that everything is bigger and better in Texas. As a member or fan of the Cowboys, it's easy to get wrapped up in that.

The Cowboys' fans expect greatness, as does everybody in the organization. A lot of people identify Dallas with the Cowboys, something that's not true of many other cities. And there are thousands of fans who live and breathe Dallas Cowboy football. Their whole week depends on a Cowboy win or loss. I know that sounds crazy, but it's part of the mystique.

I've never been around a team or a city or an environment like this. I'm glad I wasn't here in the late '80s, suffering through those lean years. It's not a fun place to be for a losing team! I'm extremely thankful that we're winners.

How to Get to the Bowl

Since a big part of being a Dallas Cowboy is the winning tradition, let's go back to Super Bowl XXX. In Chapter 1 I described some of my highlights on the field, highlights that never would have occurred without a strong commitment to football.

But life is more than football, and so is the Super Bowl. I'd like to give you an idea of what it feels like before the big game.

If you've ever played football at any level—even if it was just sandlot ball behind the schoolhouse—no doubt you have dreamed of playing in the Super Bowl. It's the biggest sporting event in the country and, except for perhaps the World Cup of Soccer and the Olympics, the biggest in the world.

Getting to this big game was the culmination of all the hard work I've put in since I first started playing football. To be privileged to play in three Super Bowls in my first four years in the league has been a phenomenal experience. There's only one word that, humanly speaking, has allowed me to reach that position, and you can probably guess what it is: Commitment.

Just to become a professional football player takes an incredible amount of commitment. And getting to the Super Bowl made me realize that all the hard work pays off. It was my reward for the countless hours I spent in off-season training, weightlifting, running, watching film, rehearsing plays and moves and strategy, or playing basketball to keep in shape and to stay agile.

Don't get the impression that I dislike all of this—in fact, I love to work out, lift weights, and do the drills that improve my game. Yet there are some aspects of being committed to football that are not so much fun. For one thing, the commitment it takes to get to the Super Bowl means spending a lot of time away from my family. Tammy and Chase are the most important people in my life and I don't like being away from them. But when training camp starts, I don't see very much of my wife and son for several weeks. That means the commitment to success goes beyond me; they need a reciprocal kind of commitment as well. Their willingness to support me in my football career is a tremendous boost when the season rolls around each summer.

But no one gets to the Super Bowl on individual and family commitment alone. Each of my teammates has to make the same commitment to the team. Our combined efforts get us through the playoffs and into the final game of the year. It can't happen unless we're all dedicated to the same goals.

A lot of big-name stars on other teams have committed themselves to excellence for their whole careers without ever making it to the Super Bowl. Guys like Reggie White of the Green Bay Packers make no apologies for saying that they'd give up the money, their Pro Bowl honors, *everything* just to play in a Super Bowl. That says a lot about what playing in a Super Bowl means.

When I joined the Cowboys in 1992, none of the Dallas players had tasted Super Bowl glory while wearing the Texas lone star on their helmets. In fact, some of them had been on the extreme other end of the scale: in Jimmy Johnson's first year as coach, the Cowboys were 1-15.

A lot of those players were still around in 1993, when we went to the Super Bowl. That tells you something very important about commitment. Commitment is a long-term deal.

Years ago, Sir Winston Churchill—the celebrated British Prime Minister who helped lead Allied forces to victory in World War II—gave a speech that I think helps define commitment. The crowd eagerly waited to hear what the great war hero and statesman would say. Surely it would be life changing, profound, and inspiring.

When at last Churchill rose to speak, he gazed deeply over his audience and intoned in a commanding voice, "Never give up. Never, never, never." And then, to everyone's bewilderment, he turned and sat down.

He had proclaimed his secret to success in six words.

The Cowboys didn't give up when they were the worst team in the NFL. They remained committed to Jimmy Johnson's program for rebuilding, and three years later they basked in the glow of the Super Bowl spotlight.

I didn't go through the bad times my teammates had to endure. I was fulfilling my military commitment while the team went from pretenders to contenders. Therefore, when I arrived for my rookie year, I walked right into a championship-caliber team.

Although I wasn't there in the lean years, I heard some of my teammates describe them all the time. They called it "Paying your dues." They talked about how tough it was to stay motivated when they rarely won. They told me how difficult it was to get up and go to work the next morning. They dreaded it. And remember, these guys had no idea that they would turn things around so soon. For all they knew, they would go 1-15 for the rest of their football careers.

But, of course, they didn't. Those players stuck with Johnson's program and saw the improvement. When that happens, you can see the light at the end of the tunnel and your commitment seems worthwhile. Probably faster than they ever dreamed, the Dallas Cowboys were again on their way to the Super Bowl.

Taking the Last Step

When the hard work and dedication pays off for your team and you make it through the final round of the playoffs still on your feet, the reality of being a Super Bowl team doesn't hit right away. In fact, it didn't hit me that first year until we were actually at the Rose Bowl in Pasadena, California. That's when it began to sink in that I was involved in something incredible.

By the time I arrived at the Super Bowl I was tired, both physically and mentally. This was a whole new experience for me. I had followed the Super Bowl my whole life and I knew it was the biggest game of a football player's career, but it had never occurred to me that for a player to get so far, he had to practice, work out, do drills, and remain in the public eye for seven months.

I always wanted to make it to the Super Bowl, but once I got there I still had to remind my body and mind that they couldn't quit yet. I had to commit myself to one more long road trip before the season is finally over.

I tried to counteract my fatigue by thinking of the Super Bowl as just another game. I didn't want my mind to blow it out of proportion. Obviously, there's most at stake when the whole world is watching, yet we were going out there to do the same things we had done in every other game—give 100 percent and run our winning strategy.

So for me, it really was just another game, the same as the rest of the season. I intended to go out and give my best effort, no matter what was at stake. It would be just me and the guy I line up against, getting back to the basics. Football at its best.

One Weird Week

So goes the theory. But it's difficult to keep that "It's just another game" perspective when the media crunch hits. That's what I dislike the most about Super Bowl week—you're hounded by the media. All the extra attention and the distractions they cause make it tough to stay focused and to concentrate. I'd much rather travel to the Super Bowl site two or three days before the game, have one media day and then play football. But the reality is this: The game is all about media coverage.

There are two media days at the Super Bowl. The first occurs in the stadium on Tuesday, our normal day off from workouts. Later in the week other times are set aside in which you're supposed to make yourself accessible to the media. We get together in a hotel banquet room furnished with a bunch of tables. Two or three players sit at each table and mobs of reporters circulate among the tables, asking the same questions over and over. In my case, they ask me incessantly what it's like to fly in combat. They ask me to compare flying with playing football. From my rookie season all the way up to the 1996 Super Bowl, the same reporters have kept asking me the same questions. Since it's a part of my job to give these interviews, I keep answering the questions.

I don't let the media attention bother me too much; there's so much about playing in the Super Bowl that I enjoy. My third appearance in the Super Bowl was different for me than the first two because I was finally a strong contributor to the team. I was playing at my position more often. I'd had a pretty good season, statistically. And with all the distractions we had throughout the season—with injuries, suspensions, and the media constantly riding our team and our players—I felt relieved to know that the season would soon be over and we could quiet a lot of critics.

For a team to enjoy success in the NFL, all sorts of personalities have to blend. The coach's job—managing everyone as a cohesive unit—is tough. Many times throughout the 1996 season we won despite ourselves. But once we beat the Packers for the conference championship, we felt relieved. Our focus quickly became the ultimate goal of the team—win the Super Bowl.

Commitment to Focus

When a team gets to the Super Bowl, there's a temptation to relax, pat yourself on the back, and say, "Hey, we made it!" Some ball clubs give in to that temptation and fail to set their sights on winning the game.

There are also other distractions besides the media blitz. Some of these are good things, but nevertheless they tempt one to lose focus. Let me tell you about the 1996 Super Bowl week and all the distractions that accompanied it.

The team flew to Arizona on Sunday, seven days before the game. Flying as a team to the game site was no different from our practice during the regular season, but arriving seven days early was unusual. During the season, we normally arrive just a day or two before the game.

Early in the week we prepared as a team, running our usual practices. We also did most of our interviews during this time.

On Thursday, our immediate families arrived on a flight chartered by the Cowboys. Also, our extended families and friends began arriving. (Eighteen friends and relatives of mine came to Tempe for Super Bowl XXX.) At this point, we could relax a little and continue to prepare for the game.

While I can't spend much time with my family and friends as I prepare for the Super Bowl, they had plenty of opportunities to entertain themselves. There's so much to do. There are Super Bowl parties, block parties, and the overall NFL hubbub. It's like an amusement park. So while my family and friends do their thing, I pretty much lay back and stay in my hotel room. I might go out to dinner, but I try to make it as normal a week as possible.

That wasn't true for Tammy; Super Bowl week was anything but normal for her. First, she had to get Chase to Tempe on her own, three days after I left Dallas. Then she stayed in a hotel room and tried to keep him happy.

(For Sunday afternoon during the game, we flew out a cousin from Iowa to baby-sit Chase. Chase is too young and too active to sit through a game. He knows that Daddy plays football, he watches the television and he'll say "Daddy, I saw you on football" when he sees me afterward. But Chase couldn't enjoy the game if he had to sit in the stadium, and then neither would Tammy. So we left Chase at the hotel to go swimming and have fun with his cousin. He didn't miss us.)

In addition to taking care of Chase during the week, Tammy felt obligated (as most of the wives did) to play hostess to our group of friends and family, making sure that everybody got where they wanted to go, that they had tickets and bus passes, and that they knew what was going on. All this activity drained her.

And, of course, there was that little matter of taking care of her husband. After seeing to all the extraneous stuff, she tried to keep me sane—to prevent me from getting too excited or losing my focus. She's a great partner in helping me prepare during the biggest football week of the year.

Super Sunday

Finally, it was Sunday. What had begun the previous July with hot, sweaty workouts had born the fruit we had committed ourselves to harvesting. This was the day we would run onto that well-groomed field in front of thousands of fans and millions in a worldwide TV audience. Today would make us champions or make this year forgettable.

Yet if you had visited the Cowboys' locker room, you wouldn't have seen a great difference between this day and any other NFL game day. The coaching staff tried to keep the same routine we followed for any other game.

We stayed in a hotel at an undisclosed location on Saturday night—just to keep away from any last-minute distractions. On Saturday evening, we attended our typical meetings (both special-teams and position meetings go over our strategies once more). On Super Bowl eve, we had a fairly early curfew and a bed check at 11:00 P.M.

Sunday morning we received standard wake-up calls—early risers at 8:00 and late people at 9:00. After breakfast, we sat through one last briefing of our game plan.

As usual, we enjoyed our team chapel service led by team chaplain John Weber. Chapel attendance is never mandatory, of course, but a bigger-than-usual crowd showed up for our pre–Super Bowl session. Attendance at that chapel reminded me of the old saying that there are no atheists in foxholes. It didn't seem to matter whether the players had any Christian background—they wanted to make sure everything was in order before the biggest game of the year.

After chapel, two buses took us to the stadium—one early bus and one late bus. The early bus arrived three hours prior to on-field warmups; the late bus showed up about an hour-and-a-half later. Then we slid into our usual routine. We went to the locker room, got dressed and taped, and waited for the magical moment when we would be summoned to the field.

Depending on what the coaches sense we need, we might get a pregame pep talk. It all depends upon the attitude of the team. If we're focused and ready to play, the coaches don't say much. But if we've had a lot of media or team distractions, the coaches make a special effort to pump us up for the game. I think their goal is to make the situation as normal as possible so we feel comfortable going into the game.

Yet no matter how casual everyone tries to be, you can sense a tension in the air. You can feel it in the coaches and the players. Everyone seems nervous, apprehensive, and a bit on edge. You can see it in their body language—guys trying to relax but finding it impossible.

And I don't see it only in others. I feel it in myself. If I don't sense butterflies in my stomach, and if I don't go to the bathroom fifteen times prior to charging onto the field, then I know I'm not ready. After playing athletics for so long, I know what that nervousness means, and I *want* that feeling. I need to channel that energy and not waste it.

That's why I go through a standard routine, even before the Super Bowl. I do everything exactly as I do it before any other game. I put my pants on the same way as always, the same leg first as always. That tells my mind that I'm going to do the same things on the field that I do during every other game.

As I sat there in the locker room in Tempe, I had to make a conscious effort to keep calm. The Super Bowl is a big game, but in this final preparation time, I have to turn my main focus on the job ahead.

Finally, the door opened.

And fifty-three guys who had spent the last seven months of their lives together headed for the opening that would lead them into the sun and into the struggle with the Pittsburgh Steelers. Each man had committed his body to the task at hand. Each had sacrificed his time, poured his heart into each game, given up his own interests for the good of the others, and vowed to do whatever it took within the rules to help his team win.

The eighty thousand people in the stands didn't know what the players were thinking as we ran onto the field. The fans didn't know how much the athletes cared for their teammates or how hard they had worked to create that team unity. The fans didn't know about the hundreds of hours each man spent in getting his body ready for this moment.

Those weren't the details the fans cared about at that moment. They didn't pay the big bucks to sit in the stands and worry about dedication and resolve. They just wanted to watch some football. They wanted to see the two best teams in the game give them sixty minutes of classic, head-to-head confrontation. The fans wanted to say that they saw a Super Bowl game well worth the money.

Of course, giving the fans what they want on Super Sunday would never be possible without one crucial factor: Commitment. Commitment is what got me into the NFL in the first place, and commitment is what got my Dallas Cowboys into the Super Bowl.

And commitment is what will motivate me to play the game as well as I can.

Working for the 'Boys . . . and the Lord

Fortunately, we won Super Bowl XXX. As a member of a wildly popular Super Bowl championship team and as a resident of the greater Dallas area,

I'm often asked to make appearances for the team. This, too, is part of my commitment to my team, a commitment every player is asked to make. Most of these appearances are relatively simple, such as appearing to sign autographs or giving radio or TV interviews.

As a member of the Cowboys, I'm in the public eye. I see that as a big responsibility and as an opportunity to further the kingdom of God. For that reason, I realize how important it is that I conduct myself not merely as an ambassador for the Dallas Cowboys, but as an ambassador for the Lord Jesus Christ. Whether I'm out to dinner with friends or going to the gas station to fill the truck with gas, people are watching me, curious to see how I conduct myself. They want to know, *Is this guy a fence-straddler or a hypocrite—or does he really live what he says he believes?*

It's a responsibility I take very seriously, and that is why I always try to keep in mind who I'm representing.

Christian groups also often request my time. After articles about me appeared in *Sports Spectrum* magazine and in *New Man* (the Promise Keepers magazine), I was bombarded with requests to speak at churches, youth groups, and other functions. My heart says, "Do them all!" but I can't. As a Dallas Cowboy, I have to make some choices. I could be as busy as I want with speaking engagements; people like to be around football players. I could probably do three or four a week, but I choose not to. I find it difficult to say no, but I've realized that sometimes I have to.

I once heard a story about a young Christian man who thought God wanted him to give his testimony to as many people as possible. Therefore he took every speaking engagement offered him. When he inevitably double-booked himself, he admitted that he had made a mistake. He realized that God didn't want him to say yes to every request, because God would not have given him two engagements on the same night. He finally understood that sometimes you have to say no.

I pray about each request I receive, evaluating the group that wants me to speak. Does it have a special need? I want to speak to people who are yearning to know God. I want to help people who need some sort of spark to anchor them in their faith. If it's just a chance for the public to shake hands with a football player, then I'm not interested.

But when given the opportunity to have a real impact on people, I get excited. For example, I was invited to speak in Cedar Rapids at a Mayor's Prayer Breakfast. I saw this as a chance to speak to several hundred people, including family and friends, and invite them to turn their lives over to Christ.

As a Cowboy, I also have an opportunity to make a lot of extra money. But I have to ask myself, "How much is it worth to sacrifice this time from my family?" The pull for material gain can be strong, but when those opportunities come, I fall back on my values and what's truly important in life: God and family. Those are the two most important things in my life, in that order. Those two things are well ahead of football or any chance to make some extra cash.

Some tremendous perks go with being a member of one of America's best-known sports teams, but I must always consider those advantages in view of my faith, my family, and my commitment to the team. I can't commit to any activity that would distract me from my relationship with God or harm my testimony for Him, to anything that would hinder my dedication to Tammy or Chase, or to anything that would hurt my ability to perform for the Cowboys.

There Is a Downside

Along with all these perks come some definite disadvantages. For one, your privacy suffers when your name is broadcasted nationwide week after week and your picture is featured in national magazines. And when you play for a team like the Cowboys—a club people either love or hate—it can be even more difficult.

It's unsettling to be hated just because you wear the Cowboys' uniform. I remember one time in Oakland, people threw beer bottles at us, made obscene gestures, and yelled profanities at us. That's about as unsettling as it gets.

But that doesn't happen only in Oakland. We get similar receptions almost everywhere we go. The Cowboys play in front of sellout crowds, at home and away, and some people come to the games just to scream at us and let us know they despise us.

Once we return home to Dallas, we get the opposite treatment—and strangely enough, that can cause difficulties, too. It can be irritating to feel that you're on display all the time, especially for someone like me, who values privacy and loves nothing more than kicking back at home with the family or playing with the kids in the front yard.

I can go to the grocery store in our town without much trouble, but I notice people looking and pointing. It's not so bad in Coppell and Valley Ranch, where we live and practice. I mow my yard and people drive by and wave. Here it's no problem, because people are accustomed to seeing the Troy Aikmans and the Emmitt Smiths.

But if Tammy and I go out and eat anywhere other than Coppell, people look over, do a double take, and then wait awhile. Finally, you'll hear them say, "It's Chad Hennings!" and approach our table with a piece of paper, asking for an autograph and saying, "This is for my son."

Again, I'm not whining. I'm not saying this is bad. I try to take it all in stride. Because of my size, people assume that I play football or basketball, then they begin to figure out who I am. I just consider it part of the job of playing for the Dallas Cowboys, part of the commitment I've made to the team. And any time kids come up to me, I sign my autograph. I'll do anything for the kids.

Another problem: Sometimes Tammy gets shuffled to the side by people who want to get to me. More than once as we've left the stadium after a game, she's been physically pushed out of the way by people frantic to get an autograph. I try to protect her from that kind of thing and she's patient with it.

There's even a downside to life in the public eye when we visit my hometown in Iowa or Tammy's hometown in Colorado. People there get excited when we visit. I'm pretty sure that the hometown folks are proud of my accomplishments, but when they see me on television, I think they look at me in a different light, as if I'm some superstar. I feel awkward around this new and different treatment. I have to remind my friends that I'm just Chad Hennings, the same small-town kid I was fifteen years ago. I'm no different from what I was then.

Still, I have nothing to complain about. The positives of being a Dallas Cowboy far outweigh the negatives. After all, I have three Super Bowl rings I can wear!

Thank You, Lord!

What Next?

When I look back on my life and review the route I've taken and the doors that have opened for me, I know that God has a purpose for me as a member of the Dallas Cowboys. I don't want to mess up what He has given me. I want to continue following His will and going wherever He wants me to go.

A lot of people ask me, "What are you going to do next?" They know, as I do, that I can't play football forever. I started later than most players, and I've already played as long as the average NFL player. So it's a legitimate question.

My answer is that I'll do whatever God wants me to do. Remember my prayer in the church in England? "Here I am, Lord. do with me what You will. Thy will be done. I'm here for Your service. Whatever You want me to do, that's what I'll do." I continue to pray that prayer every day.

When the time comes for me to retire from football, I know that God will reveal to me what He wants me to do. He'll get me wherever He wants me to be.

When my time is over with the Cowboys, I'll accept the next challenge God has for me. Perhaps I'll be able to use my notoriety as a Dallas Cowboy to influence other people for God's glory. I already sense God is leading me in that direction. But I'm committed to doing whatever God asks of me.

Whatever happens, I'm confident that playing for the Cowboys is not the end of the line for me. This blessing is the means to another goal down the road. I don't know how far that road will take me and I don't know what the end will have in store for me. But I know God will lead me to it, whatever "it" is.

That's what makes life so exciting. And that's what challenges me to keep moving ahead.

WORKOUT DRILL

1. Several of the Dallas Cowboys Chad admired as a kid are Christians: Tom Landry, Bob Lilly, and Roger Staubach, for example. When I become a fan of certain athletes, does it make a difference to me whether they're Christians? Why or why not?

2. If I were a professional athlete, how would I respond to people who would stop me on the street or approach to me in a restaurant for a chat or for my autograph? How does the example of Jesus' treatment of people affect how I think about this?

3. What famous athlete have I had a chance to meet or shake hands with? Was I impressed with him or her? Why or why not? What do I expect from famous people?

4. Am I eager to let God do whatever He wants with my life, even if it doesn't mean I get to be famous or rich?

IN A GAME AGAINST THE NEW YORK GIANTS, CHAD TESTS HIS COMMITMENT TO EXCELLENCE.

CHAPTER NINE

COMMIT YOURSELF!

Teach me your way, O Lord, and I will walk in your truth; give me
an undivided heart, that I may fear your name.

PSALM 86:11

uccess is so hard to figure. Many people have more talent than I have, yet they haven't achieved what society considers "success." Circumstances got in the way of winning the big game, getting the lucrative contract, or achieving name recognition. By contrast, others who may possess less of what society calls talent still may enjoy tremendous success.

I believe we need to rethink our definition of success. When we observe the people we consider successful versus those we consider unsuccessful, we need to look at things other than money or fame or high position. Instead, we should think about how people use what God has given them to become the best they can be. If you do that with your life, no one can ask for anything more.

But so many people don't pursue that kind of success. I feel sad when I see someone waste his or her God-given talents because of lack of commitment. And it happens all the time. Untold numbers of people never make the commitment to be the best they can be in whatever activities they choose to pursue.

You see kids failing to apply themselves at school but playing video games. And you see fathers and mothers content to work at their nine to five jobs while never realizing their potential as parents.

You might be surprised to hear that I see this kind of thing all the time even in the world of professional football. Many players—some with tremendous potential—seem happy merely to be there. They think they've got it made once they sign their contracts. They become lax and lose their focus, not realizing that the same work and pain it took to get them into the NFL is necessary for them to succeed and be the best they can be.

None of this has to happen. All of us can fully utilize our God-given talents and enjoy true success. How? By now you should be able to guess my answer: Commitment! I believe you and I can succeed in life if we make the eight commitments that follow.

1. A Commitment to Second Effort: Get Back on the Horse

In sports and other areas of life, people are throwing away their lives for unworthy pursuits. Why? Because they struggle with fully committing themselves to their goals. There are so many barriers to commitment. Here are a few of them:

- The barrier of laziness—refusing to work hard to hone God-given abilities.
- The barrier of greed—choosing to pursue goals solely for the purpose of accumulating money.
- The barrier of sin—pursuing things that are harmful to body, mind, or spirit, thus losing out on the fruits of God's plan.

I think back to my high school in Iowa. I knew some extremely talented students there. One kid in particular had fantastic speed, great athletic talent, and a fabulous arm. He was simply a great all-around athlete. He could have played college baseball or football or run college track. But he didn't. Why not? Because he refused to work at it. He didn't want to stay committed. He scorned the effort it takes to turn talent into greatness. He had a lazy tendency.

I witness the same thing in professional football. Every year in training camp I see two or three guys with the talent to make it in the NFL, but they don't succeed because they aren't committed. They don't want to work out or look at film or do the other things necessary to getting better. All these guys want is to show up at camp and brag that they play for the Cowboys. Then they visit the bars at night and tell everybody, "Hey, look at me!"

But guys like this almost always get cut from the team—if not at the end of preseason, then at midseason or at the end of the year. Although they're blessed with tremendous talent, they don't use it to the fullest. I've seen it every year that I've been in athletics.

I think their failure can be explained in one word: Fear.

Fear of work.

Fear of failure.

Fear of what others will say.

Maybe what stopped my friend in high school (besides his laziness) was the same thing that hurt me in tenth grade when I quit wrestling: the fear of failure. Maybe the pressure to do well so threatened him that he decided to bow out instead of risk not doing well.

Other friends in high school went through the same thing. They had great talent, but they found reasons not to commit to opportunities to achieve success. Maybe they felt threatened by the reputations of their older siblings. Maybe they got into a crowd of partyers and their desire for acceptance got in the way of their pursuit of greatness. Maybe they copped out by saying, "The coach doesn't like me." Maybe they were used to success coming easily to them, and when things got tough, they gave up.

Whatever their problem, all people like this ultimately have one thing in common: They're afraid to pay the price. They refuse to commit to do whatever it takes to get better.

It's so easy to quit. And once you do, it's easy to allow quitting to become a habit.

That's why you have to break the cycle. Once you've quit or failed, you have to get back on the horse and try it again. If you don't, you'll soon find something else that burns your energies. Then you'll never know if a little more effort might have made you the success you wanted to be.

The principle of committing to excellence doesn't apply only to athletics. It applies to every area of life—schoolwork, music, art, relationships. Do you want to succeed in the activities you value? Then commit to them. Work on developing the talents God has given you. Find out what is truly important in life and what God has equipped you to do, then commit yourself to it.

2. A Commitment Greater Than Sports: The Joy of Godly Living

Although I hate to see someone with athletic talent throw away opportunities because of lack of commitment, I'm not as concerned about that as I am about commitment to godly living, particularly moral purity.

We can always find people to play linebacker or point guard or goalie; but what we really need is people committed to things such as honesty, integrity, sexual purity, clean language, and caring for others. Our society needs teenagers and adults who will say that no matter what distractions come their way, they will commit themselves to living as God wants them to. This commitment is far more important than being dedicated to weight-training or practicing jump shots or throwing curve balls. There's no comparison!

Let's talk about commitment to sexual purity. I know this is a tough, tough area, especially for teenagers. Boys reach their sexual peak when they're seventeen and have a lot of hormones flying around in their bodies. And while all that is going on, society sends mixed signals. You hear one group say, "Don't have sexual intercourse until you're married." Then you hear someone else say, "You can go up to the point just prior to having sexual intercourse." (The problem with that, of course, is that once you get to that point, you *can't* put on the brakes and control your urges, let alone your partner's urges.)

Another large portion of our society shouts, "Go ahead! Have sex. Just use a condom so you don't get AIDS." No one mentions that the AIDS virus can penetrate a condom. Or that you can get other sexually transmitted diseases (STDs). Or that the possibility of getting STDs really isn't the motivation for keeping yourself sexually pure. Society sends all kinds of wrong signals.

The message you really need to listen to is one of commitment. Commit to abstaining from sex until you're married. If you're married, fulfill your com-

mitment to remaining faithful to your spouse. I know these are tough commitments in today's world where raging hormones reign and sex is so freely
depicted in movies and books. But they're vital commitments nonetheless.

When we're young, we all think we'll live forever. When we're fifteen or
sixteen years old, we think we have a lot of time before we ever have to worry
about consequences for our actions. At this point in life, it's easy to worry
more about self-gratification than about paying a price for foolish behavior.

But refusing to think about consequences doesn't mean they don't exist. I
believe we should begin early to take care of our bodies in all ways. We
should exercise, eat properly, and stay away from the drugs and alcohol. And
above all, we should abstain from sex until marriage.

I could probably preach all day on this subject, but it won't do you any
good if you don't understand commitment. God never said the Christian life
would be easy. Everyone will have troubles, but why open yourself up to
more pain by indulging in harmful activities? Why invite the spiritual and
emotional damage of getting involved in sexual impurity?

Only when you commit yourself to God will you find the dedication to
remain pure in all things. Through faith in God, you'll be able to handle the
tough challenges of sexual purity, abstaining from drugs and alcohol, and living your life with integrity. When you partner with God, you can take the
peer pressure from friends who say, "Go ahead and do it." But the only way
to stand up to that pressure is by committing yourself more to your values
than to what your friends think of you.

Imagine what would happen to our country if no one committed to
moral purity. Our country would collapse, just as every great empire has dis-
integrated which dared to abandon its commitment to high moral values.

The scary thing is, that's where our society is heading. People are no
longer committed to finding what's right and being committed to living that
way. Instead, they ask, "What can I get away with?" We're taking a dangerous
pathway when that question becomes our focus.

Not long ago, I read in our local paper that the police had arrested four
teenage kids for a car-jacking in Fort Worth. Those teens had killed three
people. The investigating detective said he had never seen more calloused

individuals in his whole life. These young people would approach people in their driveways as they left their cars, rob them, and shoot them if they resisted. Just bang, you're dead.

Kids who commit such crimes have nothing to look forward to. They have no morals. They don't know right from wrong.

Why are we heading in this direction? Pure and simple, it's because our society lacks a commitment to God's standard of right and wrong. In the name of pluralism, we have rejected the Bible as an unchanging guide to morality. Today it's like the book of Judges: "Everyone did what was right in his own eyes." And like the book of Judges, the result is moral breakdown and societal collapse.

The truth is, only the Bible presents us with God's guidelines for right and wrong. Of course it's tough to buck society and instead remain committed to moral purity. But as in most things in life, the tough road results in more success and happiness than any easy path society might offer.

Don't listen to the voices that sneer, "If you become Christians and follow God's guidelines for life, you won't have any fun." All I can say is, that is one of the greatest lies ever told. I know better!

I'm a Christian and I'm having a great time! Look at my life. Look at the things God has allowed me to do. Talk to people who know me. Why would I want to abandon that for the artificial "fun" that some people think they need? I'm already enjoying life to its fullest while avoiding all the dangers of sin!

Look at Tommy Morrison, the professional boxer. He thought he'd be happier if he had lots of women. Now he's HIV-positive and he doesn't know where his life is headed. He was in line to get a shot at becoming the heavyweight champion of the world; now he doesn't know if he's going to be around in ten years. And it wasn't as if Tommy Morrison didn't know right from wrong. He grew up in the church, he just wasn't committed to the Christian lifestyle.

Whatever other people might do, make your own commitment to living as God's Word says you should. That includes living in moral purity. It's the only way you can truly pursue happiness and success.

3. A Commitment to God's Agenda: Discovering What He Wants

As Christians, we must discover what God has in mind for us, then commit ourselves to pursuing His will.

God has a purpose and a goal set for you and He's committed to helping you fulfill that goal. Your part is to listen to Him and learn. You can choose whether you want to commit yourself to His plan or not. Just as I decided a long time ago that if I was to make it in football, I had to commit myself to a strict regimen of working out, eating right, resting, studying, and pursuing a healthy lifestyle, so you must decide that the way to true success lies in taking the path God has set for you.

Nobody made me choose the path I took. I didn't have to stay in the weightroom for so long. I didn't have to bulk up so I could withstand the rigors of the NFL season. I didn't have to push myself to become one of the strongest players on the team. But if I hadn't done so, I never would have played on three Super Bowl championship teams.

Life is like that; you get what you pay for. And if you're willing to commit yourself to a life of trusting God, you'll get rewards you never dreamed of.

Let's look at it another way. I look in the face of my little boy, Chase, and I know that he needs a father who is committed to teaching him everything he needs to know. I'd love to go ten or fifteen years down the road to see where he ends up, and then come back to be his daddy. But I can't. I must commit myself to Christ and raise Chase with God's agenda in mind. I understand it won't be easy—we'll go through sorrows, pains, and frustrations. But we'll also enjoy the happiness of being in God's will.

Another thing: we must be committed to God's plan in the "good" times as well as the "bad" times.

We have to understand that when bad things happen to good people, God is still behind the scenes. He may be trying to reveal something about Himself or trying to make us stronger.

I think about the hardships Tammy and I endured with Chase's illness. Through this, we've become a stronger family and stronger individuals. The communication between Tammy and me has improved because of it. We have a stronger bond with Chase, too. And we know that through all this, Chase will be one tough-minded young man as he's growing up.

Another part of being committed to God's agenda is commitment to His timing. To use Chase as an example once more, Tammy and I want Chase to be well *right now*. We struggled with that at first. During the first two weeks of Chase's illness, we raised the questions we've all asked during difficult times: "Why, God? Why us? What message are you trying to send us." But Jerry Lewis, the military chaplain I wrote about earlier, put the situation in perspective for us. He told us, "At times, we don't know what the will of God is for us and why we're going through something. But realize this—God loves that child more than you and Tammy could ever love him combined. And he wants nothing but the best for Chase. Hold on to that." Now we realize that it may not be in God's timing for Chase to recover quite yet. It may not be in His timing for months or a year. But Tammy and I know beyond all doubt that God loves that little boy and wants nothing but the best for him. We are convinced He will bring about His best in His timing.

We humans aren't perfect in our understanding, but we know that God has an agenda that moves along in His perfect time. Believing that is part of my commitment to God. When adversity hits, we can't bail out on our commitment. We need to do what we can and put our faith in God that He'll get us through.

It may be a roller-coaster ride, but we're committed to it.

4. A Commitment to Trusting God's Word: Knowing the Bible

In this book I've referred several times to the Bible. I hope it's a book you cherish and one that you use as your guide. I trust the Bible and base my life on it. Everything the Bible has predicted has come to pass; that's a pretty impressive track record. I know that when I read the Bible, I learn about God's agenda for the world and for my life.

Even those who don't recognize that the Bible is the inspired Word of God often use it as a basis of moral conviction. Just look at any list of moral rules and guidelines, and you will see that it reflects what the Bible says.

No matter who you are, you can read the Bible and find truth. For millennia, people around the world have based everything—from their businesses to their very lives—on the principles in the Bible. This book is God's inspired message to men and women everywhere.

One thing I learned in the Air Force and in the NFL is the value of reading instructions. In the Air Force, we had flight manuals and other instructional materials to read before we could fly. In professional football, we have the playbook, which we need to study in order to know defensive formations and what to do when we see a certain offense coming at us.

In both arenas I had to commit myself to studying and memorizing these things in order to be successful. In the Air Force, I had to know my aircraft's systems inside and out in order to prepare myself for emergency situations. If I hadn't studied my flight manual and committed it to memory, I would have crashed into the Mediterranean Sea on my very first mission. It's the same with my playbook. If I commit myself to studying it, I'll be prepared when I step onto the football field. And if I hadn't committed myself to studying my playbook—every year—I wouldn't be playing in the NFL today.

That's also the way it is with studying the Bible. When you know God's Word and commit it to memory through regular study, you'll be prepared when you face certain situations or temptations. God tells us that knowing His Word will help keep us from falling when we are tempted. Psalm 119:11 says, "I have hidden your word in my heart that I might not sin against you." That is only one of many examples in the Bible of the value of knowing what God says to us through His Word. Everything we need to know concerning the Christian life is contained in the pages of the Bible.

Knowing God's Word prepares us to do battle with the enemy, but only as we apply the Word to our lives. Satan doesn't mind a bit if you go to a Bible study or spend your personal time reading the Word, as long as you do nothing with it. But he hates it when you apply it to your life and in your ministry. And what's the best way to get the Word working in your life?

Commit it to memory, plant it in your heart. It has to become second nature so that you live it and breathe it.

God's way, as communicated to us through His Word, leads to satisfaction. It leads us to the peace and fulfillment of knowing that we're living as He wants us to. It chases away emptiness and ushers in rich, fullness of life. And that's worth far more than any amount of money, fame, or physical satisfaction the world could ever begin to offer.

5. A Commitment to Family: It's a Team Effort

Successful families are built on each member helping out the others. As I was growing up on our farm in Iowa, no one asked questions about this topic. We each had our chores to do and we did them without too much argument. A certain level of commitment was expected of my brothers, my sister, and me.

If you're a young person living at home, you need to make that same kind of commitment. You may not live on a farm, but that doesn't mean you should sit around the house and expect your mom or dad to wait on you. A family is a team, and everyone needs to play his or her part.

The father and mother earn the money and provide the instruction, discipline, and direction. The kids can help maintain the house. This might mean taking out the trash, mowing the lawn, or doing other chores. It certainly includes getting along with brothers and sisters and not causing fights.

If you are married, you must be committed to meeting your family's needs—financially, emotionally, spiritually, and in every other facet of life. You are responsible for fulfilling their needs.

You should be fully committed to your wife and meeting her physical and emotional needs. Show her your commitment by communicating with her and giving her the compassion and respect she needs as a wife and a mother.

It's the same with your children. Their physical needs must be met, but so must their emotional and spiritual needs. That means spending time with them, teaching them God's Word, praying with them, telling them you love them (in your words and in your actions), and teaching them from your life's experiences. I am so grateful that I had parents who took the time not merely to meet my physical needs (they certainly did that), but also my emotional, and spiritual needs. I wouldn't be where I am today without parents like that.

I have the opportunity to do charity work with children in the Dallas area. I visit elementary schools and high schools to talk with kids, and I've seen many examples of children who don't have that kind of commitment from their fathers. I've seen fathers who were there physically but not emotionally. I've seen situations where the parents work so many hours trying to make a living that they don't have time for their kids. And I've seen the damage that inflicts on these poor kids. It tears at my heart, knowing what many of them will have to overcome as they grow up.

Our society seems to erect a lot of barriers that keep men from being the kind of fathers we should be. Many of us find it difficult to show a lot of emotion at home. Some of us have a hard time hugging our kids, telling them that we love them when we put them to bed, and taking the time just to talk to them. That's where we husbands and fathers need to make an adjustment.

Whether you're a teenager living at home or a married man with children, a strong commitment to your family will go a long way toward deciding what kind of home you have. A committed family member, no matter what the age, will try to help maintain a peaceful, loving environment. By your example, you can find ways to encourage everyone in your family to give emotional support and love. Family relationships are give-and-take, and you can find a lot of joy by creating ways to give.

6. A Commitment to Balance: Putting Christ at the Center

Commitment isn't my only pet topic. Another one is balance. We Christians need to live balanced lives.

Illustration of cross

Here's how I illustrate it. Visualize a cross. One part of the cross is the *physical* aspect of life. This means taking care of yourself physically: working out, staying away from drugs and alcohol, eating right, avoiding sexual impurity, and so forth. Then there's the *mental* part of life. This refers to things like taking classes at school, reading books, and taking part in other activities that stimulate your thought processes. Third, you have your *family*. As a family member, you protect your emotional bonds to your family by spending time with your brothers and sisters, your parents, and other relatives. If you're married, you spend time with your wife, including getting away with her to spend some quality time without the kids. If you have children, spend time with them also, as I described in the last section. Remember, everyone in the family needs your quality time. And finally there's the community aspect. That's getting involved outside the home in Boy or Girl Scouts, church activities, Big Brothers/Big Sisters, or just sharing with others your own personal testimony.

In the center of the cross is Jesus Christ. He's there because He should be at the center of everything we do. He's the key. Everything we do must relate to Him. He's our example, our guide, our motivation, our Savior. If we put Christ in the center of our lives, we live for Him every moment of every day. In the morning, we give Him thanks for the new day. During the day, we talk to Him when we need help or when we just want to communicate with Him. When we need to make a decision, we think of what He wants us to do.

If Jesus is in the center of all that we do, the other areas of our lives will take care of themselves. If we are committed to Him and doing what He wants us to do, then the other things we dedicate ourselves to will fall into place.

The Christian life is the greatest way to live, whether you're a Dallas Cowboy, an eighth-grader, or a young father. But it's not a way of living to be taken lightly. To live as God wants you to every day means opening your heart to His leading and showing others that you love Him. It means using His Word as your guide, having fellowship with those who share a strong faith in Him, and living by Jesus' example.

It's not without its challenges. But there's no greater way to live.

7. A Commitment to Humility: The Path to Honor

In the world where I work, "humility" is not a very popular concept. How many football or basketball games have you seen where you didn't see somebody glorifying himself with a special point-scoring dance? From players mugging for the camera to tattooed rebounders turning themselves into sideshows, athletes always find new ways to draw attention to themselves.

As most football fans know, those of us who toil on the line are destined to have few opportunities to go for the glory. Some players, though, have developed a way to bring as much attention to themselves as possible. One example is the player who crashes through the line, swallows up the quarterback in his arms, deposits him flat on his back, and then proceeds to run around like he's just discovered a cure for cancer. I don't think that's the way the sport was meant to be. It's disrespectful to your opponent, to your teammates, and to the game. Unfortunately, in today's world of sports that kind of thing is accepted, almost encouraged. People want to see it.

Personally, I don't go for that kind of thing. I might put my hands together in a reference to prayer as a way of praising God, but I try to remain low-key. My philosophy is "Do it on the field and don't talk about it." When I make a good play, I don't want to make it look like it's the first time I've ever done something worthwhile. It sends the wrong message when a player brings all the attention on himself. Besides, it's a waste of energy.

Football is a team sport. Players should have a camaraderie and commitment to each other. That's not what happens when you score a touchdown, rip your helmet off, and saunter around like you're Caesar waiting for the Romans in the Coliseum to praise you. That's not a team approach.

I think that kind of behavior is a sign of arrogance and selfishness. Football players are role models, and any time we're on television, we're setting examples for young people. When you go to a high-school or junior-high game and you see kids doing the prancing bit, you know where they got it.

I'm definitely from the old school when it comes to celebrations on the field. I'm thankful that I had parents and coaches in junior high and high school who instilled in me the value of humility. Back then, I knew that if I ever did a dance on the field, I'd be finding myself a nice comfortable spot on the bench.[1]

The Bible lists humility as a valuable commodity, and I think we need to bring it back out into the open and present it as a positive alternative. I like what Solomon said in Proverbs 15:33: "The fear of the Lord teaches a man wisdom, and humility comes before honor." If we want true honor, we must be humble. Unfortunately, a lot of people have that all mixed up.

Humility is important to me because Jesus Christ, my role model, was humble. If anyone ever had anything to be proud of, it was Jesus. He hadn't just scored a touchdown or knocked down a quarterback's pass. He had created the whole world, football fields and all. He is God!

Yet he humbled Himself and came to earth to become human, just like us, so He could save us. That's like a man becoming a worm to save the worms.

That's humility!

I've talked a lot in this book about the things I've accomplished. But I don't want to draw attention to myself and make you think "Chad Hennings is a great guy." I'd prefer that you think of the great God Chad Hennings serves.

The way I see it, what I've done professionally—be it flying in the Air Force or playing for the Cowboys—is really no different than a guy going to work every morning and providing for his family. He's doing his job. It's just that I've been fortunate enough to be a fighter pilot and a football player. I realize that the ability to do those things are blessings from God. So there's nothing for me to be arrogant or prideful about.

When I'm in the spotlight, I want to be a proper role model to kids. When I do something that people like, I've always felt that the accomplishment of that task was enough praise for me. If people say, "Hey, good job," that's all the attention I need, especially if it's acknowledgement from people in my life such as my peers, my coaches, my parents, my brothers and sister, and, of course, Tammy and Chase.

If people praise you, you don't have to say, "Hey, look at me!" Doing your hard work and enjoying the success you gain through your actions should be enough. The praise that you might get is extra.

Christ said that the most humble and meek will receive the greatest rewards. Those who are great on earth will be lesser in heaven, and the lesser on earth will be greater in heaven. Knowing that helps me keep the perspective that things on earth, including attention I draw to myself, are fleeting. People who hold on too tightly to their accolades or their material things will discover that those things can vanish in a blink of an eye.

We have to have an unshakable foundation to fall back on. It can't be the praise of people, because that can disappear tomorrow. It can't be the search for fun, because that can backfire. It can't be money, because that's only temporary. It has to be a commitment to your faith, a commitment to Jesus Christ.

God wants you to maximize the skills He has given you. You may be good at public speaking, athletics, teaching, maintaining a home and family, driving a truck, digging ditches. Whatever gift you have, maximize it for the glory of God.

8. A Commitment to Stewardship: Taming the Money Monster

When I visit schools to talk with students, I usually tell them a couple of key things such as "Don't do drugs" and "Work hard at your schoolwork." But I continue to hear a scary thing from these students: "I don't care about those things. I'm going to play ball and make a lot of money." So many people seem obsessed with getting rich. They're deceived into believing that a fat bank account will solve all their problems.

The most frequent questions I get from kids deal with money. "What kind of car do you drive?" "How much money do you make?" "Let me see your Super Bowl ring. How much did it cost?" "That's a nice suit you have on. What did you pay for it?" Money issues attract young people like nothing else.

Now, I can see why people equate athletes with money. So many athletes make a big deal of the gold and glitter. Scores of them say, "I'm holding out for more money."

There's a problem with that. Such statements imply that we provide for ourselves through the contracts we negotiate. I don't think that's accurate. I prefer to say that God is taking care of me, no matter how much money I have or what level of success I achieve professionally.

As Tammy and I raise Chase, we try to show him that money is not the source of happiness. We don't buy him all the toys he wants. In fact, he has fewer toys than most of his friends. We try to show Chase how to appreciate the things that he has. We want him to learn to savor the blessings God has given us. Even though he's just a preschooler, we want him to learn these things from the start. We want him to realize that if we lost everything we have, we'd be OK. Life would still go on and we can be happy with anything.

Tammy and I try to teach him by example. We choose to live modestly; we don't acquire a bunch of material things we don't need. We don't purchase a new car every year. Of course, there's nothing wrong with money or material possessions if you have them in proper perspective. I've been blessed with the opportunity to play professional football, and I am paid good money to do it.

But when children in the schools ask me the money questions, I try to emphasize that God has blessed me with these gifts and that I'm trying to make the most of the talent He has given me. I tell them that my football career can be taken away tomorrow through an injury, so I have other things to fall back on. I have my education. I have my faith. I have a strong family bond. These things, not money, will get me through the tough times.

That way, I'm not depending on my paycheck.

Kids from poor backgrounds might look at me and say, "Oh, yeah. He's just blowing smoke because he has the money." All I can tell them is that I've never worried about money—not because I was always well-off, but because I have always trusted God to make sure I had enough to get by.

I thank God that I held a "real job" in the Air Force. I'm now making a lot more than what I made in the Air Force, but I've been happy both ways. God has always come through and He has blessed my life tremendously. I'm thankful for that. He has blessed me with a wife and a son, and He'll always be there to help me, no matter how great or small my salary becomes.

I'll be honest with you. When I first came to the Cowboys, I thought about my commitment to Jesus and how telling others about Him could negatively affect me. I said to myself, "Man, that could hurt you financially. Businesses aren't going to want to touch you. People aren't going to want to listen to you speak. People will think you're a Bible thumper." I thought about those things, but I quickly realized that it didn't matter.

I lead my life the way I do because I'm Chad Hennings, and I don't want to be a phony. I want people to look at me and say, "He's a former fighter pilot and an NFL player, but more than that he's a Christian. He's an honorable man. He has integrity. He's honest." I care more about that than what's in my bank account. It's more important to me to be true to my Lord than to have any material blessings.

You Can't Go Wrong

You can never go wrong if you commit your life to God. He is the Creator of the universe, yet He knows you personally. He has a great plan for your life, but He will reveal it to you only if you put Christ at the center of your life.

Have you committed your life to Jesus Christ? I can tell you from personal experience that there's nothing on earth more important or more worthy of your dedication! So make that commitment today. You'll never make a better decision.

WORKOUT DRILL

1. How do I define success? When I look back on my life someday, how will I know if I've been successful?

2. What has caused me to want to quit something worthwhile? Did I get back on the horse or give up?

3. What claims does God have on my body? Why should I worry about keeping it clean and pure? What have I done that has threatened to damage my body and make it unfit for God to use?

4. If people refused to be committed to each other in a family, what kind of situation would result? How committed am I to my family? Is there room for improvement? If so, how can I improve my commitment to my family?

5. Have I committed my life to Jesus Christ? Have I prayed to ask Him to forgive my sins and be my Savior? Have I told Him that I want to serve Him every day? Why or why not? Is there someone I need to talk to about this?

Endnote

1. I admit that I've dreamed of ways I'd celebrate my glory moments. I've thought through how I'd handle scoring a touchdown as a defensive lineman in the NFL. I wouldn't spike the ball. I'd walk over, hand the ball to the referee, and jog back to the bench. I'd want to retrieve the ball and keep it, but first I'd walk over and hand it to the ref. I'd do that because that's the right thing to do, pure and simple.

In 1995, I almost got the chance to test myself on this decision. It was the touchdown that got away.

We were playing the Denver Broncos and Charles Haley hit John Elway, forcing him to fumble. I jumped on the ball, picked it up, and ran toward the end zone. It was only twenty yards to the end zone and I got there untouched. I thought I had my first touchdown.

But the referees blew the play dead. They said I was down, even though nobody had touched me. I mean, I was in the clear! I felt disappointed, but I looked at the refs like "No problem." At least my team recovered the fumble and I felt I had contributed. It was my big chance, but there's always the next play, the next game, and the next season.

No matter what I accomplish on the field, I always want to give God the glory. Or to put it another, more contemporary way, I want to be a role model. I take my position in life as a professional football player very seriously, and I want to use my influence for good.

THE CROSS OF CHRIST: THE ULTIMATE SYMBOL OF COMMITMENT.

CHAPTER TEN

THE LORD JESUS CHRIST

A MAN OF COMMITMENT

*Greater love has no one than this, that he
lay down his life for his friends.*

JOHN 15:13

think often of how grateful I am to have been blessed with so many examples of commitment in my life. From the time I was a little kid growing up on an Iowa farm to our struggle with my son's illness, I have seen the difference that commitment can make in life.

I'm especially thankful for the commitment of so many people to me. It started with my parents and the unconditional love they gave me as I was growing up in the nurturing, caring environment they provided for me. They were always there for me, and that's something for which I'll never cease to thank them (and God!). My three siblings helped me to see what loving commitment really is. All of them—from my oldest brother Todd, who pushed me to be the best I could be, to my younger brother Kent to my sister Kelly—allowed me to learn what real love and commitment are. Even though we sometimes fought like cats and dogs, we always shared a great amount of love and support.

I'm also grateful to the coaches who provided the support and motivation that got me where I am today. I think of my high-school football coach, Reese Morgan, who demonstrated by both word and action what dedication and hard work can do for an athlete. He further drove home the value of commitment to me when he sacrificed his own time to make sure that the folks at the Air Force Academy had a chance to see a videotape of a raw farm kid from Iowa playing high-school football.

And, of course, there's my high-school wrestling coach, Jerry Eckenrod. He taught me so much about commitment when, without a second thought, he welcomed me back to his team during my junior year, even though I had allowed my fears to drive me out of wrestling the previous season. Without him, I never would have achieved what turned out to be my fondest memory of my high-school athletic career: my state championship. Without him, I never would have learned the crucial lessons that my hiatus from wrestling taught me.

I'm also grateful to those in the United States Air Force who demonstrated their commitment to me, especially to Coach Fisher DeBerry, who was willing to bring me on his staff as a coach but later gave me his blessing to play for the Dallas Cowboys instead.

And, of course, there's Tammy. Through everything, she has remained committed to me, first as a military wife—having to deal with my absence while living an ocean and half a continent away from her friends and family—then as a pro football player's wife. Without her loving commitment to me, there is no way I could have accomplished what I have.

But there's one other person I can't forget, a person who, as hard as it may be to imagine, has shown me more about commitment than all the people I've ever known: my heavenly Father.

The Father's Commitment

God is the very embodiment of commitment. As I grow and mature as a Christian, I see ever more clearly the awesome grandeur of God. He never changes. I know that He loves me, but I cannot fully comprehend the depth of His love and commitment for the world, for His people, for me.

That God has given me the ability to walk and breathe is an awesome miracle. Yet I know His commitment to me goes far beyond that.

As I look back over my life, I see God's hand in everything I've done, guiding me every step of the way. Even when I didn't realize it, even when I felt frustrated or discouraged by some event beyond my control, God was right there, making sure that all things came together at just the right time.

I see that so clearly now as I think about my family background and the events that led me to the Air Force Academy. I can see it in the timing of my service as a jet fighter pilot and in the timing of my coming to the Dallas Cowboys. All the time, every step along the way, God knew exactly where I needed to be in order to make me the man He was molding me to be. His timing has always been perfect. Not always comfortable, but perfect.

When I think about these things, I am overwhelmed by the evidence of God's love. But there's something else He did for me that demonstrated His love in a way I can never fully comprehend.

He sent His only Son.

In the past, when I thought about John 3:16—the verse that defines God's love for us, "For God so loved the world that he gave his one and only Son, that whoever believes in him shall not perish but have eternal life"—I supposed I was enjoying a small glimpse of how much God loved me. And I was right.

But I never really understood that love until I was blessed with the most awesome moment of my life: I became a father.

When I held my son Chase in my arms for the first time, I felt a love that I couldn't have imagined until I became a father myself. It was inconceivable to me that I could love someone with that capacity or with that intensity. I love my wife with everything that's in me, and I love my parents and brothers and sisters deeply. But the love I have for Chase is a different kind of love. It's a love for someone who I realize is actually *a part of me*. That's an incredible bond.

It was after the birth of my son that I started thinking about the sacrifice God made when He sent *His* "one and only Son" into the world for me. God did that so that I could enjoy forgiveness of sin and a new relationship with my heavenly Father. It suddenly hit me that God sent His Son to earth *knowing* that He would be persecuted, reviled, tortured, and murdered. He sent Him from the glories of heaven to the agonies of earth *knowing* that He would suffer and die a horrible, grisly, excruciating death.

I remembered that the Father made that sacrifice to redeem us, to pay a debt we could never pay. I pondered the fact that God sent His Son to die for people who scorned what He was doing for them. *And He didn't have to!* He did it because He chose to do so, not because He was somehow forced.

That's total love. That's total commitment. For us. For me!

As a father, I just couldn't fathom that. I still can't. His action is something that I could not and would not do. I could give of myself; but my son? I'm sorry, but I just can't. I won't.

God, however, *willingly* gave His Son. It was His plan, His idea.

When I think about my love for Chase, I realize there's nothing I wouldn't do for him, no sacrifice I wouldn't make. I would die for him without hesitation. I want that little boy to know how much I truly love him. I want to do everything I can to make his life comfortable and secure.

Yet I realize that my love for Chase, as consuming as it is, is as nothing compared with God's love for His Son. When I think about the day of the crucifixion—when God had to turn His back on Jesus Christ, forsake Him because He had actually become sin—I am overwhelmed with the thought of God's love for us.

It's one thing to think of my love for Chase and realize that God loves every one of us infinitely more than that. But to consider that God sent His own Son to die in our place—it's more than I can comprehend. I can understand love in human terms. But in God's terms? No way!

The Son's Commitment

Sometimes people are troubled by the fact that God sent His Son to die in our place, on our behalf. It sounds cruel to them, even perverse. How could a loving father do that to his son?

Yet they forget that the cross was also Jesus' choice. He was not the unwilling victim of a sadistic father's plot. He freely, willingly, and lovingly sacrificed His own life for us. He made this clear when He said, "No one takes [my life] from me, but I lay it down of my own accord. I have authority to lay it down and authority to take it up again. This command I received from my Father" (John 10:18).

That, friends, is commitment.

The Bible tells us that Jesus Christ was fully God, yet also fully man when He lived with us on earth. That tells me even more about the commitment God made to us though His Son.

When Jesus left His Father's side to come to earth, He was leaving an intimate relationship with the Father that had never known a moment of conflict. He did so in order to show us what true commitment really is. He continued to show us that commitment in the way He lived and in the way He died.

Everywhere Jesus went, He was committed to His followers. He demonstrated that commitment when He taught them, fed them, challenged them, healed their diseases, cast out demons, and raised the dead.

One of the stories about Jesus that most demonstrates to me His love and commitment is the account of raising Lazarus from the dead. Mary and Martha, the sisters of Lazarus, sent a messenger to Jesus to tell Him that their brother was sick. The Bible says in John 11:5 that Jesus loved Mary and Martha and Lazarus, yet He stayed where He was for two more days. Christ knew that it was God's plan for Lazarus to die.

After two days, Jesus told His disciples that they would be returning with Him to Judea. The disciples protested, reminding Him that the Jews there had tried to stone Him only a few days before. But Jesus had a commitment to keep. He intended to return to His friends in Bethany.

When Jesus finally arrived on the scene—four days after Lazarus had been buried in a tomb—He told Mary and Martha not to worry, that God would be glorified through what was about to happen. The sisters were in mourning and kept repeating, "If you had been here, my brother would not have died." But Jesus was in control. He simply told the sisters, "It's OK. I'm here. Everything's going to be fine."

Jesus then set out for the tomb. When He arrived, He directed that the stone at the mouth of the grave be removed. They protested that the body would stink by then, but He ignored them. He waited until the stone had been removed, then shouted, "Lazarus, come out!" *And he did!* The Apostle John was so astonished by what he saw that, many years later, he wrote the unlikely sentence, "The dead man came out . . ." (John 11:44). Now, dead men don't do anything; their days of "doing" are over. But this man really did come out. Just as Jesus had promised, Lazarus was alive again.

That's one of my favorite examples of Jesus keeping His word to the people He loved. Shortly after His arrival in Bethany He had told Mary and Martha that Lazarus would live. True to His word, He kept His commitment to them.

Later on, in the garden of Gethsemane, the Gospels allow us to see Jesus as He wrestled with the ultimate commitment He had made. He knew what was before Him. He knew He would be brutalized, beaten, mocked, then crucified. He knew what was coming, every detail of it. Yet He remained committed to finishing what He had started. He willingly went to the cross.

As Jesus hung suspended between earth and heaven, the Bible says that He cried out, *"Eloi, Eloi, lama sabachthani?"*—"My God, my God, why have you forsaken me?" For the first time in all eternity, Jesus was separated from His Father. God had turned His back on His only Son, because at that moment, Jesus took on the sins of the whole world. And God couldn't look on sin.

Jesus was alone. And His heart was broken.

I've thought about how I'd feel if, for some reason, I was separated from my son, even for a short time. I can't imagine what that would be like, what kind of anguish I would feel. Even in human terms it's hard to comprehend what kind of agony it would be to be forced to turn your back on your own flesh and blood.

But that's what God did for us. He turned His back on His own Son so that He could bring us into His presence. So that we could enjoy fellowship with Him. So that He could be our Father.

That's commitment!

A Measure of Commitment

When I consider all that Christ has done and continues to do for me, I am left with but one choice. How can I do anything less than commit myself completely to Him and His will for my life?

Part of my commitment to Jesus is that in everything I do, I give 100 percent. That's how I can glorify Him. Anything less than that is doing myself and my Lord a disservice. Christ gave His all for me in everything He did—from leaving the Father to dying on the cross to taking care of my needs now—so the very least I can do is give Him my all in everything I do. Not to repay Him; that would be as foolish as it was impossible. But I give Him my all because I love Him. That includes my ministries, my family, my football career, writing this book, and everything else I do. It's all His!

There is nothing more satisfying in life than doing whatever you do for the glory of God, to use your God-given talents to further His kingdom. Whether you're a preacher, a missionary, a school teacher, a fireman, an athlete, or a janitor, do what you do with every ounce of energy you have. That's how you can glorify God in your work!

I urge you to fully use your talents for the glory of God, whatever those talents might be. You don't have to be an ordained minister, an evangelist, or a missionary to serve God in what you do. We all can't be prophets or pastors, but we all have been given some talent or skill that God can use. It might be teaching a Sunday school class or leading a Bible study. Maybe it's talking with your friend or coworker about your relationship with Jesus. It could be just calling someone on the phone and talking to them about God's love. Or perhaps it's letting people know about the love of Jesus through the way you live.

However God uses you, give your all. It's a commitment that pays both current and eternal dividends.

Step-by-Step Commitment

Does it seem a little overwhelming to think of giving everything you have to Jesus Christ? I'd be the first to admit that being committed to Christ is not easy. There's no doubt it's much easier following the world's example than it is to be committed to Christ.

But this is truly a life-and-death issue. We're talking about eternity here. Not five years or ten years, but *forever*. As finite, mortal beings, we humans have trouble trying to fathom eternity. But whatever it means, it's clear that forever is a long, long time. No decision you will ever make will be more important than making a true commitment to Christ.

As your heavenly Father, God loves you. And He wants to spend time with you. He desires a commitment from you that you will be there to talk to Him. He longs for you to commit to spending time with Him in prayer, meditation, and in reading and memorizing His Word. And He wants you to commit yourself to telling others about Him.

If that sounds too difficult, then you may need to break it down into small steps. Start out by making a commitment to God Himself. Admit that you have fallen short, that you need Him, that you can't make it on your own. Believe that Jesus died for you, personally, and that He rose from the dead to win your salvation. Ask Him to come into your life and to make you a new person. That's a big commitment, but it's the most important one you'll ever make.

Then, when you're ready, commit to Him that you will read your Bible and pray for, say, ten minutes a day to start. Or that you will tell one person about your faith every day.

God knows what you can handle. It's up to you to make that commitment to Him, but He'll help you stick with it. When you became a believer in Christ, God sent His Holy Spirit into your life to empower you to keep the commitments you make. Without Him, you'd fall flat on your face. But when we depend on God's Spirit to provide the power we need, suddenly the world opens up. Commitment becomes a joy, not sheer duty.

As you grow in the Lord, He'll help you to commit to bigger and better things. He'll give you more and more frequent opportunities to serve Him, and you'll see Him at work in ways that will blow your mind. It's quite an adventure!

Maybe it would help to look at it as though you were training for athletic competition. At first, you may be out of practice and out of shape. There's no way you can play in the game right now, and no one expects you to. But you know if you stay committed and continue to train, you'll eventually be able to compete . . . and win!

It's the same thing with being a Christian. You can't expect to become some kind of prayer warrior or evangelist overnight. You have to take the small steps toward spiritual maturity. As you take those small steps you'll get in better and better shape spiritually. Before long, you'll find yourself having a more effective prayer life as well as more boldness to tell others about your faith.

Remember what I wrote about my reluctance to talk to other people about Jesus (chapter 6)? I had committed my life to Christ at the time, yet I still had to take small steps to learn how to witness to others. I started out talking to small groups and eventually I became comfortable speaking to a thousand people at a time. Now, I love to tell others about Jesus Christ!

That's why I know that taking small steps of commitment works. I'm a living example.

So take those small steps. Take them with a heart of commitment. If you commit yourself to praying for a half-hour a day or to witnessing to one person, follow through on your commitment with the best effort you can muster.

And make use of the time God has given you! Your time is precious to God, so utilize each day, committing your time to Him. As it says in Psalm 90:12, "Teach us to number our days aright, that we may gain a heart of wisdom."

Spiritual growth is a process, and some people mature more quickly than others. That's something I've learned as I've walked with Jesus. But I've made a commitment to Him that I'll do whatever it takes to be in His will. I tell God every day, "Here I am, Lord. do with me what You will. Thy will be done. I'm here for Your service. Whatever You want me to do, that's what I'm going to do."

I'm committed to Jesus Christ. I'm committed to knowing Him and doing His will for my life. I'm committed to doing everything I can to gain a deeper knowledge of Him and to bringing others into a relationship with Him. I'm committed to living my life the way He wants me to.

I'm committed to being like Him! And I hope you are, too.

WORKOUT DRILL

1. Think of people in your life who have been examples of commitment. In what ways did they demonstrate that commitment?

2. Have you ever thought of God as your greatest example of commitment? If so, in what specific ways do you recognize that He's committed to you? If not, why not?

3. If you're a father, have you ever considered the depth of God's love for you in sending His only Son to die in your place? How do you respond to that kind of love? Why?

4. Think of some small steps you could take as commitments to God. How can you take those steps today?

A CHAD HENNINGS PROFILE

Chad at Home

Hometown: Coppell, Texas
Wife: Tammy
Son: Chase

Hobbies: Tropical fish (the aquarium in the Hennings home holds several species of beautiful, exotic, saltwater fish). Watching John Wayne movies (Chad has a life-sized cutout photo of The Duke that stands in one corner of the family room).

Next-door neighbor: Paul Frase, who plays in the NFL for the Jacksonville Jaguars.

The Incredible Hulk

Chad Hennings is one of the strongest football players in the National Football League. Here is the tale of the tape:

Height: 6 feet 6 inches
Weight: 290 pounds

(Chad's weight varies, depending on the time of the year. He likes to start the season at 295 because the wear and tear of the NFL causes him to lose weight throughout the season.)

Bench press: 530 pounds
Squat: 700 pounds

Big Man on Campus

Chad attended Benton Community High School in Van Horne, Iowa. Benton Community was a fairly small high school, but Chad made a big impression, both in the classroom and in sports. Here's a list of his honors:

- Finished in the top five of his class
- Member of the National Honor Society
- Boys' State Senator for Iowa at Boys State
- Captain of the football and wrestling teams
- All-conference in football
- All-state in football
- Three-year letter winner in football
- State champion in wrestling
- Competed in 4-H
- Involved in peer counseling

The Academy Proudly Presents

After graduating from high school, Chad went west. From the plains of Iowa, he traveled to the mountains of Colorado, entering the Air Force Academy in 1984. While there, he racked up a collection of honors as long as the Academy's trainer pilot runway:

- Twice named Academic All-American
- On Superintendent's List (GPA and military performance above 3.0) all four years
- Unanimous All-American selection in football as a senior
- Conference Defensive Player of the Year as a senior
- Won the Outland Trophy as the top defensive lineman in college football as a senior
- Stan Bates Academic Award winner
- Appeared on *The Bob Hope Christmas Special*
- Appeared on *The Today Show* with Bryant Gumbel

- Named Most Inspirational Player, Japan Bowl
- Selected captain of his team in the East-West Shrine Game
- Selected Most Valuable Football Player and Athlete at the Air Force Academy

Off We Go into the Wild, Blue Yonder

Chad's military commitment didn't end after his four-year hitch at the Academy. Next, he was off to flight school and the possibility of several more years in a United States Air Force uniform instead of an NFL uniform.

While serving in the Air Force, Captain Chad Hennings received many awards, including the following:

- Selected to attend the Euro-Nato Joint Jet Pilot Training Program (ENJJPT)
- Graduated from the ENJJPT and was selected to fly the A-10 Tankbuster, also called the Warthog.
- Flew 45 combat missions in Desert Storm and Operation: Provide Comfort in the 1991 Persian Gulf Conflict.
- Logged 900 hours of jet flying time.
- Received Air Force Achievement Medal, Unit Commendation, and Humanitarian Medal. Also was awarded Thunderbolt Safety Award for emergency landing of his A-10 during his initial flight to Turkey to fly in Desert Storm.
- Currently serves as a liaison officer in the Air Force.

This Cowboy Rides Tall!

Chad Hennings' timing is fantastic. He was in the military at just the right time to use his piloting skills to help the Kurds in Iraq. And as a football player, he joined the Cowboys just when they were ready to rejoin the elite teams of the NFL. As a result, Hennings won three Super Bowl rings in the first four years he was in the league.

But Chad doesn't wear those rings all the time. That's not his style.

Instead, he wears them mostly when he speaks to groups—especially to kids. Among the groups Chad has addressed are the Air Force Academy Football Banquet, Prayer Breakfasts at different Air Force bases including the Air Force Academy, an Athletes in Action Banquet at the Super Bowl, a National Council on Youth Leadership, and numerous high school assemblies for Athletes in Action.

COWBOY TRADITION

Dallas Cowboys in the Pro Football Hall of Fame

NAME	YEAR	POSITION	NOTE
Bob Lilly	1980	Defensive tackle	First college player drafted by 'Boys
Roger Staubach	1985	Quarterback	Led team to two Super Bowl wins
Tom Landry	1990	Coach	Won 270 games and two Super Bowls
Tex Schramm	1991	President	Built team into Super Bowl champs
Tony Dorsett	1994	Running back	All-time leading Cowboys' rusher
Randy White	1994	Defensive tackle	A nine-time Pro Bowl player

Cowboys All-Time Leaders

Rushing	Tony Dorsett	12,036	yards
Receiving	Drew Pearson	7,822	yards
Passing	Roger Staubach	22,700	yards
Scoring	Rafael Septien	874	points
Interceptions	Mel Renfro	52	interceptions
Most seasons	Ed Jones	15	seasons
Most games	Ed Jones	224	games
Sacks	Harvey Martin	113	sacks
Solo Tackles	Lee Roy Jordan	743	tackles

Top Performances

Largest margin of victory	56-7 vs. Eagles,	10 - 9- 66
Top rushing effort	Emmitt Smith, 237 yards vs. Eagles	10-31- 93
Top passing effort	Don Meredith, 460 yards vs. 49ers	11-10- 63
Top receiving	Bob Hayes, 246 yards vs. Redskins	11-13- 66
Longest run from scrim.	Tony Dorsett, 99 yards vs. Vikings	1 - 3- 83
Longest pass	Don Meredith, 95 yards vs. Redskins	11-13- 66
Longest punt	Ron Widby, 84 yards vs. Saints	11 - 3- 68
Longest punt return	Dennis Morgan, 98 yards vs. Cards	10-13- 74
Longest fumble return	Chuck Howley, 97 yards vs. Falcons	10 - 2- 66

Attendance Notes

- From October 16, 1977, through December 21, 1982, the Cowboys sold out their home stadium for 44 straight games.
- The largest home crowd in Cowboy history was 80,259 on November 24, 1966.
- Between the Cowboys' opening season in 1960 and the end of the 1995 season, they had played before almost 15 million fans at home and more than 15 million fans on the road.
- The smallest crowd ever for a Cowboys' home game was 10,000 against the San Francisco 49ers on November 20, 1960.
- On August 15, 1994, the Cowboys played the Houston Oilers in front of 112,376 fans in Mexico City.

A Place in the Sun

The Dallas Cowboys have trained at St. Edward's University in Austin, Texas, since 1990. Each year about 100,000 fans turn out to watch the 'Boys go through their summer practice sessions and their scrimmages.

The fans get an extra bonus when they visit St. Edward's. Each day of camp features Autograph Alley, which allows fans to get close to the players for their signatures. Other features of training camp include the Cowboys' Golf Tournament and the annual Blue-White intrasquad scrimmage.

THE BIBLE SPEAKS ABOUT COMMITMENT

ough talk from Jesus about commitment: "If anyone comes to me and does not hate his father and mother, his wife and children, his brothers and sisters—yes, even his own life—he cannot be my disciple" (Luke 14:26).

Jesus' demand for total commitment: "Then he said to them all: 'If anyone would come after me, he must deny himself and take up his cross daily and follow me' " (Luke 9:23).

The ultimate commitment: "Therefore, I urge you brothers, in view of God's mercy, to offer your bodies as living sacrifices, holy and pleasing to God—this is your spiritual act of worship" (Romans 12:1).

No wimps need apply: "Do not be afraid of what you are about to suffer. I tell you, the devil will put some of you in prison to test you, and you will suffer persecution for ten days. Be faithful, even to the point of death, and I will give you the crown of life" (Revelation 2:10).